Lecture Notes in Economics and Mathematical Systems

385

Javier Gardeazabal Marta Regúlez

The Monetary Model of Exchange Rates and Cointegration

Estimation, Testing and Prediction

Springer-Verlag
Berlin Heidelberg New York
London Paris Tokyo
Hong Kong Barcelona
Budapest

Authors

Dr. Javier Gardeazabal
Dr. Marta Regúlez
Instituto de Economía Pública
Universidad del País Vasco
48940 Lejona-Vizcaya, Spain

ISBN-13: 978-3-540-55635-0 e-ISBN-13: 978-3-642-48858-0
DOI: 10.1007/978-3-642-48858-0

Typesetting: Camera ready by author/editor

42/3140-543210 - Printed on acid-free paper

A Oscar

PREFACE

This monograph is the result of merging parts of the authors's doctoral dissertations presented at The University of Pennsylvania in the spring of 1991.

We would like to thank the members of our dissertation committees, Francis X. Diebold, Roberto S. Mariano and Marc Nerlove for their guidance and helpful comments. We received very good comments from Albert Ando, Yin-Wong Cheung, William English, Søren Johansen, W. Krelle, Bruce Mizrach and seminar participants at the University of Pennsylvania and the XV *Simposio de Análisis Económico* in Barcelona. Our thanks also to Werner A. Müller of Springer-Verlag for his help. Of course, any remaining errors are ours.

We are indebted to *Departamento de Trabajo del Gobierno Vasco* and the Department of Economics at the University of Pennsylvania for financial support through our graduate studies. The research underlying this work was partially supported by two Alfred P. Sloan Foundation Fellowships.

We could not have written this monograph without the support received from our families.

Sections within chapters are numbered using roman numerals. References to equations within the same chapter are of the form (II.7) whereas if they correspond to different chapters are (2.IV.4).

TABLE OF CONTENTS

Chapter 1. Introduction

These notes draw from the Theory of Cointegration and use it in order to test the monetary model of exchange rate determination. The analysis is empirical, that is, we take a theoretical model of exchange rate determination and asses its empirical performance. We have also addressed several issues concerning to the Theory of Cointegration.

The starting point is the monetary model. Its several versions give rise to different equations of exchange rate determination. They express the domestic currency value of a unit of foreign currency as a linear combination of differentials between domestic and foreign fundamentals. These fundamentals are money supplies, interest rates, national incomes, etc.

These models have been tested in many occasions. The impression one gets from these studies is that the monetary model does not capture the short run dynamics of the exchange rate, specially when assessed in terms of forecasting accuracy. Meese and Rogoff (1983) compared the forecasting performance of the monetary models of exchange rate determination with that of time series models, the forward rate and the random walk. The naive random walk beats the other models. However, even though those equations of exchange rate determination may be bad indicators of how exchange rates are determined in the short run, they could still describe long run equilibrium relationships between the exchange rate and its fundamentals.

The concept of long run equilibrium relationship is borrowed from the theory of cointegration. In plain words, we say that various nonstationary time series are cointegrated when linear combinations of them are stationary. Stationary deviations from those long run relationships are allowed in the short run.

In the empirical tests of monetary models they look for a set of regressors that explain a high percentage of exchange rate variability and, at the same time, leave a white noise disturbance. In addition, they usually omit any consideration to the nonstationarity of several of the variables involved. The theory of cointegration takes into account the nonstationarity and looks for a stationary, possibly correlated over time, disturbance.

This monograph also focuses on the issue of optimal prediction in partially nonstationary multivariate time series models. In particular, we carry out an exchange rate prediction exercise.

The type of nonstationarity allowed for is somehow restrictive. We assume that stationarity of a p-dimensional time series can be obtained by taking first differences of all its components. However, by doing so, we will generally introduce some unit roots in the moving average representation of the differenced time series. This is so because the number of *unit roots*, d, is smaller than its dimension. In this sense the time series is partially nonstationary. The d unit roots are shared by all the elements of the vector time series and we will say that the p univariate time series have d *common stochastic trends*. The difference between the dimension of the system and the number of common trends, $r = p - d$, is the number of *cointegrating vectors* or stationary linear combinations of the individual time series. The Theory of Cointegration treats these cointegrating vectors as long run static equilibrium relationships from which the p variables deviate temporarily in the short run. In terms of exchange rate determination, the long run relationships determine the long run value of the exchange rate.

The rest of the analysis is organized as follows:

Chapter 2 describes several versions of the monetary model. All the discussion in this chapter is by now in the textbooks of International Monetary Theory (see for instance Baillie and McMahon (1990)). However, we felt that a short discussion of the old monetary models would not hurt and, furthermore, improve these notes by making them self contained.

In chapters 3 to 5 and 9 we test the monetary model as a long run approximation for mark, pound and yen, US dollar rates.

Chapter 3 introduces some definitions, and presents evidence on the nonstationary character of the variables involved in the monetary model. We use the unit root tests developed by Dickey and Fuller (1979), Phillips (1987) and Phillips and Perron (1988) in order to determine whether a given time series is stationary in levels, first differences or trend stationary. We find that the variables that are considered as fundamental determinants of the exchange rate have different kinds of nonstationarity. That is, some are stationary in levels, some in first differences and some others trend stationary.

We also analyze the stationarity of the difference between domestic and foreign fundamentals. That is, we look for cointegration between pairs of fundamentals with a known cointegrating vector using Engle and Granger (1987) methodology. We find that, in general, foreign and domestic fundamentals are not cointegrated, at least when we impose a particular cointegrating vector.

We have reviewed several pieces of empirical evidence on the long run character of the monetary equations of exchange rate determination and its building blocks (purchasing power parity, money demands) using the theory of cointegration. The existing evidence in the literature is mixed and crucially depends on the methodology used. If the procedure developed by Engle and Granger (1987) is used, the results point towards the nonexistence of long run equilibrium relationships. However, if Johansen's (1988) methodology is employed, the results are the opposite. The chapter ends with a discussion of how this apparent paradox can be explained.

Chapter 4 tests the monetary model within the framework of the theory of cointegration using Johansen (1988, 1991a) methodology. It presents several tests of the restrictions implied by the monetary model. The empirical evidence points towards the existence of several long run equilibrium relationships that link the exchange rate and its fundamentals. These long run relationships are not trivial in a sense to be made precise below. None of the variables is excluded from all the equilibrium relationships. Finally, they do not satisfy the usual symmetry restrictions imposed in most theoretical monetary models.

Chapter 5 studies the short run dynamics of the exchange rate. The monetary models introduced in chapter 2 can be cast in the asset market specification. In this chapter, we show how one can derive the asset market view model from a cointegrated multivariate time series model of the type used in chapter 4. The validity of the asset market view model depends on some restrictions on the parameters of the model. These restrictions imply the weak exogeneity of the exchange rate. We present these tests and comment on the implications for short run exchange rate dynamics.

Chapter 6 studies the small sample distribution of the likelihood ratio test statistics used in chapters 4 and 5 under deviations from normality. Disturbances are drawn from six probability distributions (Cauchy, Student's t, Uniform, Normal, a nonsymetric distribution and ARCH). The nominal sizes of the tests are found to be quite robust to departures from normality except for the cases of Cauchy disturbances. The empirical power of the likelihood ratio test for the number of cointegrating vectors is very low only when there are ARCH effects, remaining high under other types of deviations from normality.

In chapter 7 we give two different interpretations of the time series model and describe several estimation procedures. On the one hand, the system can be viewed as the reduced form of a simultaneous equations model. On the other, it also admits a common trends representation that is important in order to analyze its forecasting properties. Different methods of estimation are selected to estimate the ECM under alternative sets of restrictions on the short and long run parameters of the model.

The properties of forecasts generated by cointegrated systems are studied in chapter 8. The vector of h-step-ahead forecasts will satisfy the cointegration relations exactly in the long run. This property of the forecasts generated by the cointegrated system implies that when we forecast with the ECM, the error correction term becomes negligible for a large enough forecasting horizon. In this chapter we cast the ECM into a state space form. This representation is useful to derive the optimal forecast and the asymptotic covariance matrix of the vector prediction error.

Chapter 9 deals with nominal exchange rate prediction of mark, pound and yen, US dollar rates. We use the monetary approach to exchange rate determination in order to specify a nine dimensional VAR. Estimation of the model is carried out under different assumptions regarding the long and short run parameters. As indicators of forecasting performance we use the mean error, mean absolute error, root mean squared error and Theil's U statistic. This last measure uses the random walk as the benchmark model. When no restrictions are imposed, at no horizon does any of the estimated models beat the random walk. When restrictions on the short run parameters are imposed, at short horizons the estimated models outperform the random walk. The restrictions in the long run parameters also help predicting the mark / dollar exchange rate.

In chapter 10 we analyze the small sample properties of the forecasts generated by a cointegrated system. We specify a bivariate Data Generating Process (DGP) with a single unit root and therefore one cointegrating vector. The model is estimated by various methods, namely, Johansen's maximum likelihood estimator, Engle and Granger's two step procedure and the OLS estimator of the system when the number of unit roots is misspecified. The two misspecified models assume the number of unit roots to be equal to zero (VAR in levels) or two (VAR in first differences).

Finally, chapter 11 concludes.

Chapter 2. The Monetary Model of Exchange Rate Determination

I. Introduction

Monetary models of exchange rate determination were developed after the collapse of the fixed exchange rate system in the early 70's. They are descendants of the Mundell-Fleming type of models. Several versions have been put forward giving rise to three main types of models. These are the *flexible price* monetary model due to Frenkel (1976) and Bilson (1978), the *sticky price / real interest rate differential* of Dornbusch (1976) and Frankel (1979) and the *sticky price-asset* monetary model of Hooper and Morton (1982). The modeling strategy is similar in all cases. Ad hoc aggregate macroeconomic relationships are used to obtain a semi-reduced form equation that specifies the level of the exchange rate as a linear function of *fundamentals*[1].

All these monetary models, and others, can be cast into what Mussa (1984) has called the *asset market view* model of exchange rate determination. The new element in this approach is that it views foreign exchange as an asset an therefore prices it as any other asset, that is, in a forward looking fashion. This generalization allows for the inclusion of non-observables among the fundamentals.

Today this *asset market view* is the state of the art in exchange rate modeling despite the little empirical evidence in favor.

---

1 The specification is log-linear.

The new literature on *Target Zones* that arose after Krugman's (1988) seminal paper, uses as starting point the *asset market view* model.

In the following pages we overview the monetary and asset-market models of exchange rate determination. Then, we review some pieces of empirical evidence and point out some of the shortcomings and virtues of those theoretical models.

II. Monetary Models

All monetary models of exchange rate determination are based on two building blocks. Namely, money demands and purchasing power parity (PPP). Thus, failure of any of the parts brings about the collapse of the monetary model.

In order to introduce these models and their individual components let us define the following notation:

m_t = nominal stock of money,

p_t = price level,

y_t = real national income,

i_t = nominal rate of interest,

π_t = inflation rate,

f_t = one period forward exchange rate,

a_t = current account balance,

q_t = real exchange rate,

s_t = spot nominal exchange rate, the price of foreign currency in terms of domestic currency.

All variables are expressed in logarithms, except the interest rates which are in levels. All the variables defined above refer to the *home* or *domestic* country, the *foreign* counterparts are denoted with a star.

There are two building blocks that are common to all monetary models:

a) Demands for real monetary balances,

$$m_t^d - p_t = -\alpha - \beta y_t - \gamma i_t, \qquad (II.1)$$

$$m_t^{*d} - p_t^* = -\alpha^* - \beta^* y_t^* - \gamma^* i_t^*, \qquad (II.2)$$

where β (β^*) is the domestic (foreign) income elasticity and γ (γ^*) the domestic (foreign) interest rate semi-elasticity of the demand for money. Thus, the demands for real monetary balances are postulated to be linear functions of national incomes and interest rates. One can think of these interest rates as the market rates on risk free one period bonds. Equilibrium in the domestic and foreign money markets is described by the equilibrium conditions,

$$m_t^d = m_t^s = m_t, \quad m_t^{*d} = m_t^{*s} = m_t^*. \qquad (II.3)$$

National incomes are assumed to be at their full employment levels.

b) The PPP relation is at the basis of the monetary approach since it is used in order to link domestic and foreign money demands. Its simplest form is,

$$p_t = s_t + p_t^*. \qquad (II.4)$$

Which expresses domestic prices as the cost in domestic currency of foreign goods. Prices are assumed to adjust so that foreign and domestic goods markets clear instantaneously.

With these two basic ingredients one can form the simplest equation of exchange rate determination. Let us use (II.1), (II.2),

(II.3) and, as in most of the theoretical and empirical work, assume $\beta = \beta^*$ and $\gamma = \gamma^*$. Solving for the exchange rate we get,

$$s_t = (\alpha - \alpha^*) + (m_t - m_t^*) + \beta\,(y_t - y_t^*) + \gamma\,(i_t - i_t^*). \qquad \text{(II.5)}$$

In words, the exchange rate gets determined as a linear combination of the differences between domestic and foreign fundamentals.

Equation (II.5) is in itself representative of the *flexible price* monetary models. Using the so called *covered interest parity* (CIP),

$$f_t - s_t = i_t - i_t^* \qquad \text{(II.6)}$$

one can derive Bilson's (1978) equation of exchange rate determination,

$$s_t = (\alpha - \alpha^*) + (m_t - m_t^*) + \beta\,(y_t - y_t^*) + \gamma\,(f_t - s_t). \qquad \text{(II.7)}$$

Note that (II.5) and (II.7) are basically equivalent in a world with perfect capital mobility since CIP is simply a *no-arbitrage* condition whose violation would imply the possibility of infinite capital gains.

Another element of the class of *flexible price* monetary models is derived from a weaker version of the PPP relation, the *ex-ante relative purchasing power parity*,

$$E_t(s_{t+1} - s_t) = E_t(\pi_{t+1} - \pi_{t+1}^*), \qquad \text{(II.8)}$$

where $E_t\pi_{t+1} = E_t(p_{t+1} - p_t)$ and $E_t\pi_{t+1}^* = E_t(p_{t+1}^* - p_t^*)$ are the expected inflation rates conditional on all available information at time t. Equation (II.8) together with the *uncovered interest parity* (UIP),

$$E_t(s_{t+1} - s_t) = i_t - i_t^*, \qquad \text{(II.9)}$$

and equation (II.5) give,

$$s_t = (\alpha - \alpha^*) + (m_t - m_t^*) + \beta\,(y_t - y_t^*) + \gamma\, E_t(\pi_{t+1} - \pi_{t+1}^*). \qquad (II.10)$$

So far we have derived three different equations of exchange rate determination within the *flexible price* model of the type postulated by Frenkel(1976) and Bilson (1978). Any of them expresses (the log of) the exchange rate as a linear function of differentials of (the log of) domestic and foreign fundamentals.

In this kind of models, adjustment takes place instantaneously. However, in the type of models analyzed by Dornbusch (1976) and Frankel (1979, 1984) the adjustment to the equilibrium is slow due to price stickiness.

Thus, the two-country world is assumed to be in equilibrium only in the long run. In the short run, however, prices deviate from their equilibrium values. The other variables, money demands, national incomes and interest rates are assumed to adjust instantaneously. PPP is assumed to hold only in the long run,

$$\bar{s}_t = \bar{p}_t - \bar{p}_t^*,$$

where the upper bar denotes the *long run* value of that variable. Thus, equation (II.10) gives the long run value of the exchange rate as,

$$\bar{s}_t = (\alpha - \alpha^*) + (m_t - m_t^*) + \beta\,(y_t - y_t^*) + \gamma\, E_t(\bar{\pi}_{t+1} - \bar{\pi}_{t+1}^*). \qquad (II.11)$$

Expectations are formed according to the rule,

$$E_t(s_{t+1} - s_t) = \theta\,(s_t - \bar{s}_t) + E_t(\bar{\pi}_{t+1} - \bar{\pi}_{t+1}^*). \qquad (II.12)$$

The expected depreciation equals a proportion of the gap between the exchange rate and its long run value plus the expected long run inflation differential. Using the UIP (II.9), the expectations rule

(II.12) and equation (II.11) one obtains,

$$s_t = \alpha_0 + (m_t - m_t^*) + \beta(y_t - y_t^*) + \delta E_t(\bar{\pi}_{t+1} - \bar{\pi}_{t+1}^*) + \lambda(i_t - i_t^*), \qquad \text{(II.13)}$$

where $\alpha_0 = (\alpha - \alpha^*)$, $\delta = \gamma - (1/\theta)$ and $\lambda = 1/\theta$. The reason why this model is called *real interest rate differential* monetary model is because equation (II.13) can be rearranged so as to have both the nominal and real interest rate differentials as right hand side variables, that is, as fundamental determinants of the exchange rate.

The last monetary model that we analyze is the sticky price-asset model of Hooper and Morton (1982). A simplified version of their model assumes that the *long run real exchange rate*,

$$\bar{q}_t = \bar{s}_t - \bar{p}_t + \bar{p}_t^*, \qquad \text{(II.14)}$$

is determined by domestic and foreign cumulated current account balances,

$$\bar{q}_t = \phi \sum_{i=0}^{t} a_i + \psi \sum_{i=0}^{t} a_i^*. \qquad \text{(II.15)}$$

One way of thinking about this last equation is by simply considering the dependence of the trade balance (which accounts for the largest part of the current account) on the terms of trade, which in a monetary economy equals the real exchange rate.

The new exchange rate equation can be derived from (II.13), (II.14) and (II.15) as,

$$s_t = \alpha_0 + (m_t - m_t^*) + \beta(y_t - y_t^*) + \delta E_t(\bar{\pi}_{t+1} - \bar{\pi}_{t+1}^*)$$

$$+ \lambda(i_t - i_t^*) + \phi \sum_{i=0}^{t} a_i + \psi \sum_{i=0}^{t} a_i^*. \qquad \text{(II.16)}$$

This equation is one of the most general exchange rate equations that has been derived in the literature and with it we finish our brief exposition of monetary models.

III. The Asset Market View

The monetary models described above give rise to equations of exchange rate determination such as (II.5), (II.13) and (II.16). Any of these equations involve the nominal interest rate differential, which in turn is linked to the expected change in the exchange rate through the UIP relationship. Thus, substituting (II.9) in any of the exchange rate equations we can write,

$$s_t = k_t + \eta\, E_t(s_{t+1} - s_t), \tag{III.1}$$

where k_t is a linear combination of fundamentals. If we had started with equation (II.5) then,

$$k_t = (\alpha - \alpha^*) + (m_t - m_t^*) + \beta\, (y_t - y_t^*)$$

and $\eta = \gamma$. If, on the other hand, the initial monetary equation was (II.13), then

$$k_t = \alpha_0 + (m_t - m_t^*) + \beta\, (y_t - y_t^*) + \delta\, E_t(\pi_{t+1} - \pi_{t+1}^*).$$

Finally, the exchange rate equation (II.16) implies,

$$k_t = \alpha_0 + (m_t - m_t^*) + \beta\, (y_t - y_t^*) + \delta\, E_t(\bar{\pi}_{t+1} - \bar{\pi}_{t+1}^*) + \phi \sum_{i=0}^{t} a_i + \psi \sum_{i=0}^{t} a_i^*.$$

More generally, people think of equation (III.1) as nesting not only monetary models but many others too. Mussa (1983) points out that there are many unobservable variables that can be considered as direct determinants of exchange rates; "There is no easy way to quantify the effects on expectations of a speech by the governor of a central bank or a rumor of a shift in preferences for national monies by large holders of liquid reserves.". Thus, one can think of k_t as aggregating all observable and nonobservable fundamental determinants of the exchange rate. The way this aggregation takes place is not, however, specified.

One of the more interesting characteristic of the asset market view is that it satisfies the three requirements of Mussa (1983) that a good exchange rate model should satisfy. Namely, the exchange rate is related to current values of the fundamentals and expected values of itself, the expectations are rational and, finally, the expectations of future values of the exchange rate and its determinants are related to observable variables when the asset market model is derived from a monetary model.

The stochastic difference equation (III.1) can be solved forward to get,

$$s_t = \frac{1}{1+\eta} \sum_{i=0}^{\infty} \left(\frac{\eta}{1+\eta} \right)^i E_t(k_{t+i}), \qquad \text{(III.2)}$$

where we have ruled out any bubble term. This forward solution can be used to derive an equilibrium value of the exchange rate provided we assume some sort of stochastic process for the fundamentals. If we assume that fundamentals, in absence of intervention, follow a driftless random walk,

$$k_{t+1} = k_t + \varepsilon_{t+1}, \qquad \text{(III.3)}$$

where $\varepsilon_t \sim$ iid $(0,\sigma_\varepsilon^2)$, then $E_t(k_{t+i}) = k_t \;\forall\; i \geq 0$. Therefore, the exchange rate is uniquely determined by fundamentals, $s_t = k_t$, where k_t

can be defined as any of the functions above or it may also include additional terms. The exchange rate is then determined by the fundamentals and at the same time it follows a random walk,

$$s_{t+1} = s_t + \varepsilon_{t+1}.$$

This formulation of exchange rate movements is consistent with the observed random walk behavior of exchange rates as the evidence presented by Meese and Singleton (1982) shows.

It is precisely on this exchange rate model, or rather its continuous time analog, that the recent models of *target zones* are based. This growing literature includes Krugman (1988), Miller (1988), Klein (1989), Froot and Obstfeld (1989a, 1989b), Svenson (1989) and Delgado and Dumas (1990) among others. Using the asset market view they derive the solution for the exchange rate when the central banks intervene and therefore change the value of the fundamentals.

IV. Empirical Evidence

Frenkel (1976), Bilson (1978), Frankel (1979, 1984) Hooper and Morton (1982) in their original papers present empirical evidence that can be considered as favoring their models. Their assessment is based on the multiple correlation coefficient and the comparison of estimated coefficients with the expected sign as predicted from their theories.

Besides the original papers there is a considerable amount of studies that have tested the monetary model and its building blocks (see Levich (1985), Hodrick (1987), Diebold (1988) and Baillie and McMahon (1990) for more references).

Meese and Rogoff (1983) have used monetary equations of

exchange rate determination in order to predict out of sample values of the exchange rate. The forecasts that the monetary approach yields perform badly when compared with pure time series models, in particular the simple random walk. This is so even when forecasts are based on actual values of the right hand side variables. One possibility is that deviations from PPP and/or UIP may account, at least partially, for the poor performance of monetary models. That is, real exchange rates and risk premia may be important determinants of the exchange rate. Another reason could be an incorrect specification of the demand for money in either of the countries, specially their dynamics, and, of course, the restrictions imposed by assuming identical parameters in both demand functions.

Later empirical studies such as Woo (1985) and Wolff (1987) have improved the forecasting performance of monetary models by including lagged values of the exchange rate as explanatory variables and postulating unconstrained VAR systems for the regressors of the exchange rate equation. This points out that the dynamics of the exchange rate monetary models were severely restricted in the original models and therefore as soon as we allow for a richer dynamic structure the fit is better.

V. Treatment of Nonstationary Variables

The empirical work reviewed so far is based on the assumption of stationarity. In fact, many of the variables involve in monetary models are nonstationary as reported by Meese and Singleton (1982) for exchange rates and Nelson and Plosser (1982) for several macroeconomic magnitudes. Researchers proceeded in two possible directions, they either omitted any consideration to the nonstationary character of the data or simply took care of it by either working with first differences of the original variables or the residuals from regressions on deterministic time polynomials.

As it will be seen below, such a treatment of nonstationary variables is clearly suboptimal. On the one hand, it is important to correctly specify whether those variables are trend or difference stationary (see Nelson and Plosser (1982)). If we assume them to be difference stationary and inference is based on regressions on the levels of the variables, standard asymptotic theory does not apply. On the other hand, if the nonstationarity is removed by differencing, then we could be ignoring very important long run information.

That is why we think that there is still room for further investigation on the validity of the old monetary models. In our analysis we will model the nonstationarity in an optimal manner. In addition, the methodology we use below allows for much richer dynamics with a clear cut distinction between long run and short run dynamics. Finally, it does not impose the symmetry restrictions between domestic and foreign fundamentals.

Chapter 3. Long Run Exchange Rate Determination I

I. Introduction

International Monetary Theory postulates a number of relationships among macroeconomic variables of different countries. Examples are, absolute and relative Purchasing Power Parity (PPP), Real Interest rate Parity (RIP), Uncovered Interest Parity (UIP) and (forward) foreign exchange market efficiency. These international linkages are at the basis of the economic modeling of open economies, in particular, monetary models of exchange rate determination, despite the fact that many authors have found empirical evidence against them.

Cumby and Obstfeld (1984) presented indication of deviations from PPP and RIP. Hodrick (1987) has surveyed the literature on the efficiency of the forward rate, the evidence is less conclusive in this case. Meese and Rogoff (1983) found poor out of sample fit of structural models of exchange rate determination. These references are just the tip of the iceberg-size literature on each of the preceding subjects.

In the light of these empirical findings, theoretical models ought to be amended so that they take into account the deviations from those postulated international linkages. The time series properties of such deviations, as well as those of the variables themselves, are of crucial importance. If those deviations are stationary they have a temporary character whereas nonstationary deviations from macroeconomic relationships have a permanent effect. This in turn implies that when deviations are temporary there is still hope for a long run relationship.

The postulated international linkages are specified as linear combinations of, typically, nonstationary macroeconomic variables. In general, a linear combination of nonstationary variables is nonstationary too, but when such a combination is stationary the case for a long run relationship can be made. Otherwise, spurious contemporaneous correlation among macroeconomic variables may be found because they are all driven by independent stochastic trends[1]. When such a stationary linear combination of nonstationary variables exists we say that the variables are cointegrated. The notion of cointegration was introduced by Granger (1981) and the literature has been surveyed by Hendry (1986) and Engle (1987).

Our view of the monetary model allows for the possibility of cointegration between the exchange rate and its fundamentals. Thus, the cointegrating relationships can be interpreted as equations of long run exchange rate determination. In the short run, however, the exchange rate will deviate from its long run value.

In this chapter we present some evidence on this direction using the methodology developed by Engle and Granger (1987). We will discuss the advantages and problems that one finds using this methodology.

With the development of cointegration theory a number of international macroeconomic relationships, that were rejected as reflection of short run equilibria, have been revived. So far, most of the empirical literature focuses on the estimation of a single cointegrating vector using the two-step procedure of Engle and Granger.

---

1 See Phillips (1986).

Studies of cointegration and PPP are those by Corbae and Ouliaris (1988), Gubitz (1988), Thom (1989), Enders (1988, 1989) and Mark (1990). In the context of foreign exchange market efficiency Lucey (1988), Hakkio and Rush (1989) and MacDonald and Taylor (1989) are some examples. Monetary models of exchange rate determination were tested by Boothe and Glassman (1987) and Baillie and Selover (1987).

The organization of this chapter is as follows. Section II introduces some definitions and the procedure proposed by Engle and Granger (1987). Section III motivates the analysis of exchange rate determination in the context of cointegration by analyzing an old type of regression equation that has been the focal point of many empirical studies in international economics. We reexamine the results obtained by Frankel (1984) in the light of the recent developments in the theory of cointegration. In section IV we describe Engle and Granger's procedure and the way we have implemented it. In sections V we use data on pound, yen and marc dollar rates and macroeconomic fundamentals of the US, UK, Japan and Germany. We analyze the stationarity of the variables under study using unit root tests. For this purpose we use Dickey and Fuller (1979), Phillips (1987) and Phillips and Perron (1988) tests for unit roots. In this section we also carry out some tests for unit roots in the univariate time series representation of the difference between domestic and foreign fundamentals. These are in fact tests for a special form of cointegration between fundamentals. For example, we analyze whether domestic and foreign supplies are cointegrated with cointegrating vector (1, -1). The section also includes tests for cointegration between the exchange rate and its fundamentals using the residual based tests statistics whose asymptotic distributions have been tabulated by Phillips and Ouliaris (1990).

II. Some Preliminary Definitions and Engle and Granger Procedure

For the time being we will use Engle and Granger's definition of cointegration which in turn requires a few preliminary definitions.

Definition 1: A scalar time series x_t is said to be *covariance stationary* if both its mean $\mu = E(x_t)$ and its autocovariance function $\gamma(h) = E(x_t - \mu)(x_{t-h} - \mu)$ do not depend on t.

Remark 1: If a p-dimensional time series is covariance stationary, all p individual components are individually so. The converse is not true.

Definition 3: Integrated Process.

A scalar time series x_t is said to be *integrated of order d*, I(d), if it has a stationary, invertible ARMA representation after differencing d times.

Definition 4: Cointegrated Time Series.

A vector process X_t is said to be *cointegrated*, if all individual components of X_t are individually I(1) but there exists a vector β such that the linear combination $z_t = \beta' X_t$ is I(0). The vector β is called the cointegrating vector.

The Engle and Granger procedure of modeling cointegrated time series is very simple. First, one tests for the degree of integration of individual variables. If all variables are integrated of order one we then proceed to estimate the, assumed unique, cointegrating vector by

OLS applied to the so called cointegrating regression. The residuals of that regression should be stationary if the regresand and the regressors are cointegrated. In order to test for stationarity of the residuals, standard unit root tests are used. However, since the residuals are estimated this makes a difference in terms of the asymptotic distribution of the test statistics. If the null of no cointegration is rejected, then one can estimate an *error correction model* (ECM) that takes into account the short run dynamics of all the variables included in the cointegrating regression. This ECM can be written as,

$$\Delta X_t = \alpha\, z_{t-1} + \Gamma(L)\, \Delta X_{t-1} + \varepsilon_t, \qquad (II.1)$$

where each variable in X_t adjusts to the cointegrating error z_{t-1}, that can then be interpreted as a disequilibrium error.

It is interesting to note that the OLS estimator of the cointegrating vector is consistent (see Phillips and Durlauf (1986) and Stock (1987)) even in the presence of simultaneity bias.

III. Interpretation of Previous Results in terms of The Theory of Cointegration

Let us consider the monetary equation (2.II.11) derived in chapter 2 and interpret it as a *cointegrating regression* model. For this purpose we assume that after substituting the expected value of the inflation differential for its current value, (2.II.11) obtains up to a stochastic disturbance u_t, not necessarily serially uncorrelated. Thus the cointegrating regression is,

$$s_t = \beta_0 + \beta_1\,(m_t - m_t^*) + \beta_2\,(y_t - y_t^*) + \beta_3\,(i_t - i_t^*)$$

$$+ \beta_4 (\pi_t - \pi_t^*) + u_t. \qquad (III.1)$$

Using data on yen, marc, sterling pound, frech franc and canadian dollar *viv a vis* US dollar rates, M1, industrial production, money market interest rates and actual inflation rates, Frankel (1984) reports estimates of equation (III.1) for five exchange rates. These results are partially reproduced in table I of Appendix A. Frankel concludes, "....the presence of wrong signs.....and the predominance of low significance levels render the results discouraging for the monetary equation.".

Seven years later and in the light of the theory of cointegration, the results reported in table I can be interpreted in a different manner. Suppose that all the regressors and the regresand in the monetary equation (III.1) are I(1), whereas u_t is a stationary process, I(0). Then, the variables in the equation are said to be cointegrated. The vector $\beta = [1, -\beta_0, -\beta_1, -\beta_2, -\beta_3, -\beta_4]'$ would then be the cointegrating vector. Therefore, a unit root in the OLS residuals would imply the rejection of the hypothesis of cointegration.

OLS estimates of equation (I.1) were not reported by Frankel. In fact, the regressions in table I were estimated using the Cochrane-Orcutt method and the coefficient ρ reported in the table corresponds to the parameter of the AR(1) process fitted to the residuals. Although it is by no means a formal test for a unit root in the OLS residuals, one would conjecture that those residuals are not stationary, since the estimated ρ coefficients are so close to one. If this were the case, the exchange rates considered would not be cointegrated with their respective sets of fundamentals. This, in turn, may be explained in two different ways. On the one hand, equation

(III.1) could be interpreted as a *spurious* regression and therefore the exchange rate is not cointegrated with its fundamentals. On the other, we could simply be leaving out a nonstationary fundamental determinant of the exchange rate which would be captured by the disturbance term.

Meese and Rogoff's conjecture that the poor forecasting performance of structural models of rate determination could be due to the simultaneity bias introduced by the OLS estimation technique can also be reexamined. As Engle and Granger (1987) point out and Stock (1987) shows, in a cointegrating regression OLS gives consistent estimates of the parameters even in the presence of simultaneity bias. This is so because the covariance among the regressors and the disturbance term is of a lower order in T than the variance of the regressors[2] and the convergence to the true value is even faster than standard econometric estimates.

On the other hand, Meese and Rogoff used in their forecasting exercise VAR models whose elements were the regresand and the regressor in (III.1). If the exchange rate and its fundamentals were cointegrated, they could have obtained better long run predictions, imposing in the estimated VAR the restrictions implied by the cointegrating relations. In chapter 9 we exploit this.

Formal tests of cointegration between exchange rates and their fundamentals are carried out in the following sections.

---

2 If the regressors are I(1) then, their variance goes to infinity as $T \longrightarrow \infty$.

IV. Testing for Cointegration Using Engle and Granger Methodology

In this section, we describe the estimation and testing procedures used in the empirical application described in the following section.

Using the definition of cointegration given by Engle and Granger (1987), the exchange rate and the fundamentals should all be integrated of order one as univariate processes. Therefore, if we follow this definition, the first step would be to test for the existence of unit roots in the univariate representation of all the variables. In doing so we will make use of the tests developed by Dickey and Fuller (1979), Phillips (1987) and Phillips and Perron (1988). The augmented Dickey Fuller (ADF), Phillips' $Z(\alpha)$ and $Z(t_\alpha)$ test statistics were calculated for different specifications. Diebold and Nerlove (1990) have surveyed this literature.

The ADF tests were computed as the t-statistic of the coefficient associated with y_{t-1} in the following regressions:

$$\text{i) } \Delta y_t = \alpha\, y_{t-1} + \sum_{j=1}^{p} \delta_j \Delta y_{t-j} + \varepsilon_t$$

$$\text{ii) } \Delta y_t = \mu + \alpha\, y_{t-1} + \sum_{j=1}^{p} \delta_j \Delta y_{t-j} + \varepsilon_t$$

$$\text{iii) } \Delta y_t = \mu + \beta\, t + \alpha\, y_{t-1} + \sum_{j=1}^{p} \delta_j \Delta y_{t-j} + \varepsilon_t .$$

The disturbance term ε_t is assumed to be white noise.

Phillips' $Z(\alpha)$ and $Z(t_\alpha)$ test statistics were extended by Phillips and Perron for the the case of an autoregression with fitted drift and the case of an autoregression with fitted drift and trend. The $Z(\alpha)$ and $Z(t_\alpha)$ statistics are computed 'corrected' normalized bias and t statistics associated with y_{t-1} in the following regressions:

i) $y_t = \hat{\alpha}\, y_{t-1} + \hat{u}_t$

ii) $y_t = \tilde{\mu} + \tilde{\alpha}\, y_{t-1} + \tilde{u}_t$

iii) $y_t = \bar{\mu} + \bar{\beta}\,(t - T/2) + \bar{\alpha}\, y_{t-1} + \bar{u}_t$.

For exposition let us consider case ii). The normalized bias is given by $T(\tilde{\alpha} - 1)$ and the 'corrected' normalized bias is,

$$Z(\alpha) = T(\tilde{\alpha} - 1) - (\tilde{\lambda}/m_{yy})/2,$$

where $\tilde{\lambda} = (\tilde{\sigma}^2_{Tl} - \tilde{s}^2)/2$, $m_{yy} = \sum_{t=1}^{T}(y_t - \bar{y})^2$, $\bar{y}$ = sample mean, $\tilde{s}$ is the standard error from the residual in ii) and,

$$\tilde{\sigma}^2_{Tl} = \left(\sum_{t=1}^{T}\tilde{u}^2_t + 2\sum_{s=1}^{l} w_{sl}\left(\sum_{t=s+1}^{T}\tilde{u}_t\tilde{u}_{t-s}\right)\right) / T,$$

where $w_{sl} = 1 - s/(l+1)$. The corrected t-stat is given by,

$$Z(t_{\alpha}) = (\tilde{s}/\tilde{\sigma}_{Tl})\, t_{\tilde{\alpha}} - \tilde{\lambda}'\tilde{\sigma}_{Tl}/m_{yy}^{-1/2},$$

where $\tilde{\lambda}' = \tilde{\lambda}/\tilde{\sigma}^2_{Tl}$. For the definition of the $Z(\alpha)$ and $Z(t_{\alpha})$ test statistics when the model is (i) see Phillips (1987) and for the model (iii) see Phillips and Perron (1988).

Phillips and Perron show that the limiting distribution of the $Z(\alpha)$ and $Z(t_{\alpha})$ statistics are invariant within a wide class of weakly dependent and possibly heterogeneously distributed innovations $\{u_t\}$. They also show that it is the same as the original untransformed Dickey-Fuller statistics under the assumption of iid errors, so that the tables derived by Fuller (1976) may be used.

The second step in testing for cointegration is estimation of the cointegrating regression. Engle and Granger suggest the OLS estimator because this naive estimator minimizes the residual variance of the cointegrating relation so that it picks the linear combination of the variables that is most likely to be stationary. Note that this argument relies on the assumption that there is only one cointegrating vector.

The last step is to test for a unit root in the residuals estimated from the cointegrating regression. We use the ADF, $Z(\alpha)$ and $Z(t_{\alpha})$ tests statistics as described by Phillips and Ouliaris (1990). They derive and tabulate the asymptotic distribution of these statistics under the null hypothesis of no cointegration. These limiting distributions are different from the original one tabulated by Fuller (1976) and depend on the number of variables involved in the cointegrating regression.

V. Empirical Results

In this section, we test for cointegration between various US$ exchange rates (German Mark, Japanese Yen and British Pound *vis a vis* the US Dollar, thus the US is always considered as the foreign country) and their corresponding fundamentals. These are measured as foreign and domestic money supplies, indexes of industrial production, interest rates and inflation rates. The sample period goes from January 1974 to December 1989. The data is described in the Data Appendix.

We first test for the degree of integration of the variables individually and also in relative form, i.e. $(m - m^*)$, $(y - y^*)$, $(i - i^*)$ and $(\pi - \pi^*)$. Notice that when we test for a unit root in the time series representation of $(m - m^*)$, we are in fact testing for no cointegration between domestic and foreign logarithms of money supplies. Rejection of the unit root hypothesis implies that m and m^* are cointegrated with cointegrating vector (1, -1)'. Since the cointegrating vector is known, the asymptotic distribution of the unit root tests are the ones tabulated in Fuller (1976). Acceptance of the null hypothesis does not rule out the possibility that a different linear combination of m an m^* could be stationary. The same argument applies to $(y - y^*)$, $(i - i^*)$ and $(\pi - \pi^*)$.

The results of these tests are presented in tables II.a, II.b and II.c of appendix B. These tables indicate which of the test statistics are significant, i.e. reject the null hypothesis of a unit root, at various significance levels. They also show whether domestic and foreign fundamentals are cointegrated. The results for Germany / US indicate that inflation and interest rates differentials may be considered as stationary and therefore be cointegrated, whereas the exchange rate, relative national incomes and money supplies seem to be nonstationary. The statistics for Japan / US strongly reject the hypothesis of nonstationarity of relative outputs and inflation differentials and provide weaker evidence of stationarity in the case of the exchange rate, relative money supplies and interest rate differentials. All the UK / US time series seem to have a unit root except for the inflation differential.

Since we have found that some of the variables in the model can be better described as stationary rather than nonstationary, the Engle and Granger methodology is not directly applicable. Some authors proceed to test for cointegration only when all the variables are integrated of order one, eliminating the possibility of cointegration when some variables are stationary.

A wider definition of cointegration, however, allows for some of the individual variables to be stationary in levels. Cointegration defined in terms of a p-dimensional array X_t requires $b'X_t$ to be stationary although X_t is nonstationary as a vector process while ΔX_t is stationary[3]. Trivial cointegrating vectors may now appear, since onecan always form a linear combination of a stationary variable and a nonstationary one that assigns a unit coefficient to the former and a zero coefficient to the latter. This definition of cointegration gives more flexibility to the analysis and is the concept used by Johansen (1988a) and Phillips and Ouliaris (1990).

Having this definition of cointegration in mind, we now proceed to test for cointegration using some of the residual based tests discussed by Phillips and Ouliaris (1990). Table III reports the outcome of the cointegrating regression (III.1) for Germany, UK and Japan versus the US. The residuals from those regressions are then tested for the presence of unit roots using the $Z(t_\alpha)$, $Z(\alpha)$ and ADF statistics. Tables IV.a, IV.b and IV.c summarize these tests statistics. The null hypothesis of no cointegration is not rejected at any reasonable significance level. Does this imply that there is not even a single cointegrating vector among those variables? The answer is no. As we have seen above, some of the fundamental determinants of exchange rates appear to be stationary and, therefore, trivial cointegrating vectors should exist. It seems that residual based tests for cointegration are

---

3 Note that the nonstationarity of a multivariate time series does not imply that each of its univariate components should be nonstationary.

not powerful enough to capture them. In fact, the OLS estimator used in Engle and Granger's procedure has been found to have important small sample bias by Gonzalo (1989) and Banerjee et al. (1986). This small sample bias of the OLS estimator together with the low power of standard unit root tests may be the reason why we do not reject the null of no cointegration.

We have also considered the following unrestricted cointegrating regression,

$$s = \beta_0 + \beta_1 m + \beta_2 m^* + \beta_3 y + \beta_4 y^* + \beta_5 i + \beta_6 i^* + \beta_7 \pi + \beta_8 \pi^* + u, \qquad (III.2)$$

where the time subscript has been suppressed. A deterministic time trend was also allowed for as another specification of the cointegrating regression.

Tables V.a, V.b, V.c and V.d. report test for unit roots in univariate time series representation of the fundamentals as they appear in (III.2). Nonstationarity of money supplies is strongly rejected for all the countries. Inflation seems to be stationary for all countries but the US. The series of Industrial production appear to be stationary about a deterministic trend. The other variables, seem to be nonstationary. Our previous finding that some of the domestic and foreign fundamentals were cointegrated, comes from the fact that those fundamentals where stationary at the univariate level.

Table VI presents the cointegrating regressions. Even though no formal tests of restrictions on the coefficients are made, one would say that they seem to be different enough so that the cross country restrictions are not satisfied[4]. Tables VI.a VI.b and VI.c summarize the tests for cointegration based on the residuals from the regressions in table VI. The asymptotic distribution of the residual based tests for cointegration depend on the number of regressors in the cointegrating regression. Phillips and Ouliaris (1990) have tabulated the asymptotic distribution of the residual based tests only for the case of up to 5 regressors whereas the cointegrating regression III.2 includes 8 regressors. However, on the basis of those tables one can see that critical values rise, for a given significance level, with the number of regressors. The test statistics reported in tables VI.a-VI.c are almost always smaller than the critical values for the case of five regressors. Then, we can accept the null hypothesis of no cointegration.

VI. Conclusions

According to the evidence presented so far, the monetary approach to exchange rate determination does not hold even as a long run approximation. Exchange rate deviations from its fundamentals are nonstationary. On the other hand, many authors[5] have found evidence

---

4 Note that if we were to formally test these restrictions on the cointegrating vector, then we would have to generate the asymptotic distribution of the OLS estimator of the cointegrating vector that is not standard. However, in the next chapter we formally tests those restrictions using likelihood ratio tests.

5 Corbae and Ouliaris (1988), Gubitz (1988), Thom (1989), Enders (1988, 1989) and Mark (1990).

against the existence of cointegration between exchange rates and price differentials as PPP would predict. To the extent that PPP stands as a keystone in the construction of monetary equations of exchange rate determination one would not expect to find cointegration between exchange rates and its fundamentals, unless one includes real exchange rates as an extra fundamental.

However, the methodology used so far is not well designed for dealing with situations in which there are more than one cointegrating vector and when the variables involved have different degrees of integration. The methodology used in the next chapter is capable of handling those cases.

APPENDIX A

Table I: Monetary Equation. Frankel (1984).

	Constant	$(m-m^*)$	$(y-y^*)$	$(\pi-\pi^*)$	$(i-i^*)$	ρ
Germany	.80	-.05	.07	1.34	-.61	.95
	(.21)	(.33)	(.22)	(.82)	(.27)	
France	1.34	.17	-.23	2.41	-.24	.81
	(.07)	(.17)	(.13)	(.69)	(.24)	
U.K.	-.20	.12	-.13	-.06	-.28	.97
	(.61)	(.22)	(.17)	(.05)	(.21)	
Japan	4.39	.21	.27	.53	-.40	.98
	(1.0)	(.20)	(.23)	(.33)	(.27)	
Canada	.44	.08	.18	-.48	-.27	.98
	(.32)	(.12)	(.12)	(.32)	(.17)	

Source: Frankel (1984) Table 7.1. Reproduced with permission of the author and The University of Chicago Press, National Bureau of Economic Research.

Table II.a.- Unit Root Tests. Germany/ US.

		s	$(m-m^*)$	$(y-y^*)$	$(\pi-\pi^*)$	$(i-i^*)$
ADF p=4	τ	-1.18	-0.59	-1.59	-3.38 (a)	-2.04 (c)
	τ_μ	-1.31	-1.20	-1.62	-5.20 (a)	-4.02 (a)
	τ_τ	-1.45	-2.48	-3.07	-5.45 (a)	-3.85 (b)
ADF p=12	τ	-1.06	-0.62	-1.48	-1.03	-1.62 (d)
	τ_μ	-1.81	-2.22	-1.53	-1.89	-3.68 (a)
	τ_τ	-2.01	-3.51 (c)	-3.43 (c)	-2.14	-3.18 (d)
Z_α	$\hat{\alpha}$	-0.79	-0.16	-1.42	-25.63 (a)	-3.40
	$\tilde{\alpha}$	-1.39	-1.29	-1.19	-51.75 (a)	-8.63
	$\bar{\alpha}$	-5.48	-18.7 (d)	-52.7 (a)	-129.2 (a)	-51.2 (a)
$Z(t_\alpha)$	$\hat{\alpha}$	-3.18	-1.42	-3.5	-8.09 (a)	-1.84
	$\tilde{\alpha}$	-1.20	-1.52	-1.57	-11.74 (a)	-3.21
	$\bar{\alpha}$	-4.30	-17.9 (d)	-21.8 (c)	-27.81 (a)	-16.8

a = significant at the 1 % level, b = significant at the 2.5 % level,

c = significant at the 5 % level, d = significant at the 10 % level.

Table II.b. Unit Root Tests. Japan / US.

		s	$(m-m^*)$	$(y-y^*)$	$(\pi-\pi^*)$	$(i-i^*)$
ADF p=4	τ	-1.16	-0.19	-0.98	-4.65[a]	-2.07[c]
	τ_μ	-0.83	-1.24	-0.94	-4.95[a]	-2.44
	τ_τ	-2.07	-3.04	-4.48[a]	-5.18[a]	-2.62
ADF p=12	τ	-0.88	-0.35	-0.40	-2.14[c]	-1.59
	τ_μ	-1.27	-0.84	-0.30[d]	-2.46	-1.96
	τ_τ	-2.73	-2.67	-3.87[a]	-2.07	-2.13
Z_α	$\hat{\alpha}$	-0.14	0.02	0.19	-78.64[a]	-1.80
	$\tilde{\alpha}$	0.28[c]	-2.96	0.35[c]	-80.30[a]	-2.24
	$\bar{\alpha}$	-5.2	-27.9[b]	-19.2[d]	-187.4[a]	-11.0
$Z(t_\alpha)$	$\hat{\alpha}$	-4.06	0.93	0.17	-29.89[a]	-0.96
	$\tilde{\alpha}$	0.41	-2.48	0.30[c]	-30.27[a]	-1.12
	$\bar{\alpha}$	-4.29	-19.0[d]	-8.32	-60.17[a]	-4.54

Table 2.c. Unit Root Tests UK / US.

		s	$(m-m^*)$	$(y-y^*)$	$(\pi-\pi^*)$	$(i-i^*)$
ADF p=4	τ	-0.96	-3.85	-1.35	-4.09[a]	-1.84
	τ_μ	-1.66	-0.99	-1.58	-5.04[a]	-2.88
	τ_τ	-1.42	-2.25	-2.92	-6.04[a]	-2.85
ADF p=12	τ	-0.89	-2.84[a]	-0.99	-1.59[a]	-1.22
	τ_μ	-1.93	-1.22	-1.13	-2.17[a]	-2.34
	τ_τ	-2.12	-2.82	-3.68	-3.08[a]	-2.34
Z_α	$\hat{\alpha}$	-0.53	-0.39	-1.63	-45.17[a]	-1.93
	$\tilde{\alpha}$	-1.25	0.45[c]	-1.12	-60.67[a]	-5.94
	$\bar{\alpha}$	-3.46	-18.76[d]	-20.8[c]	-146.9[a]	-21.3[c]
$Z(t_\alpha)$	$\hat{\alpha}$	-2.04	-12.07	-3.09	-11.90[a]	-0.74
	$\tilde{\alpha}$	-1.52	1.53	-1.11	-13.25[a]	-.743
	$\bar{\alpha}$	-2.93	-11.17	-10.32	-28.96[a]	-3.10[d]

Table III. Cointegrating Regressions. Restricted Model.

$$s = \beta_0 + \beta_1 t + \beta_2(\bar{m} - \bar{m}^*) + \beta_3(\bar{y} - \bar{y}^*) + \beta_4(i - i^*) + \beta_5(\bar{\pi} - \bar{\pi}^*) + u$$

	β_0	β_1	β_2	β_3	β_4	β_5	R^2	DW
Germany	.	.	-0.97	1.43	-1.26	7.15	0.23	0.21
	0.16	.	-0.77	1.24	-0.79	7.82	0.23	0.19
	0.58	-0.003	-0.94	-0.58	-1.02	10.50	0.34	0.23
Japan	.	.	1.08	-0.77	3.06	4.24	0.55	0.23
	0.47	.	0.98	-0.88	2.99	4.18	0.55	0.22
	2.86	-0.004	0.61	1.57	0.98	-0.13	0.74	0.14
UK	.	.	-1.57	-7.55	6.09	0.15	.	0.21
	-8.82	.	0.32	-0.73	1.00	0.16	0.46	0.06
	-5.90	-0.005	-0.50	-0.09	0.81	-0.59	0.51	0.06

Table IV. Residual Based Tests for Cointegration.

Table IV.a. Germany / US.

	ADF(4)	ADF(12)	Z_{α}	Z_t
Standard	-2.36	-2.38	-1.83	-1.08
Demeaned	-2.25	-2.29	-1.39	-0.82
Demeaned and Detrended	-2.34	-2.36	-2.78	-1.52

Table IV.b. Japan / US.

	ADF(4)	ADF(12)	Z_{α}	Z_t
Standard	-1.97	-1.68	-5.01	-3.01
Demeaned	-1.89	-1.71	-4.42	-2.78
Demeaned and Detrended	-2.45	-2.36	-2.15	-1.06

Table IV.c. UK / US.

	ADF(4)	ADF(12)	Z_{α}	Z_t
Standard	-2.62	-3.44	-2.67	-1.42
Demeaned	-1.27	-2.04	0.98	0.89
Demeaned and Detrended	-1.56	-2.46	0.43	0.36

Table V.a. Tests for unit roots. Germany.

		m	y	π	i
ADF p=4	τ	6.05[a]	-0.79	-3.09[a]	-1.42
	τ_μ	-0.82[c]	-0.16[d]	-4.85[a]	-2.63[d]
	τ_τ	-1.91	-2.12	-5.65[a]	-2.39
ADF p=12	τ	1.95[b]	-1.11	-1.85[d]	-1.36
	τ_μ	-1.31	-0.59[d]	-2.05	-3.23[b]
	τ_τ	-3.47[c]	-2.80	-1.78	-3.03
Z_α	$\hat{\alpha}$	0.23	0.32	-11.6[a]	0.07
	$\tilde{\alpha}$	-0.07[c]	2.02[a]	-34.9[a]	-2.50
	$\bar{\alpha}$	-26.1[b]	-24.4[b]	-123.[a]	-25.0[b]
$Z(t_\alpha)$	$\hat{\alpha}$	13.9[a]	0.54	-5.23[a]	0.13
	$\tilde{\alpha}$	-0.27[d]	2.93[a]	-8.98[a]	-1.67
	$\bar{\alpha}$	-17.1[a]	-18.1[a]	-25.0[a]	-16.4[a]

Table V.b. Tests for Unit Roots. Japan.

		m	y	π	i
ADF p=4	τ	4.48[a]	-0.93	-3.54[a]	-1.36
	τ_μ	-1.79	0.06[c]	-4.20[a]	-2.58[d]
	τ_τ	-2.47	-4.82[a]	-5.31[a]	-2.70
ADF p=12	τ	3.32[a]	-1.02	-2.43[b]	-1.44
	τ_μ	-2.18	0.21[c]	-2.37	-3.25[b]
	τ_τ	-2.30	-5.26[a]	-2.39	-3.74[b]
Z_α	$\hat{\alpha}$	0.11	-0.87	-33.6[a]	0.05
	$\tilde{\alpha}$	-1.42	1.08[a]	-53.4[a]	-0.93
	$\bar{\alpha}$	-48.3[a]	-8.63	-176.[a]	-6.42
$Z(t_\alpha)$	$\hat{\alpha}$	11.4[a]	-4.25[a]	-19.5[a]	0.11
	$\tilde{\alpha}$	-4.34[a]	-3.95[a]	-23.3[a]	-0.80
	$\bar{\alpha}$	-28.7[a]	-8.71[a]	-51.7[a]	-4.40[a]

Table V.c. Tests for Unit Roots. UK.

		m	y	π	i
	τ	6.49[a]	-1.13	-2.07[c]	-.049
ADF	τ_μ	1.29[a]	-.69	-3.67[a]	-2.65[d]
p=4	τ_τ	-1.21[d]	-2.33	-5.61[a]	-2.60
	τ	2.73[a]	-1.53	-0.97	-0.38
ADF	τ_μ	0.31[b]	-0.74	-1.69	-2.96[c]
p=12	τ_τ	-2.03	-1.86	-3.44[c]	-2.94
	$\hat{\alpha}$	0.63	-0.39	-7.80[a]	0.26
Z_α	$\tilde{\alpha}$	0.55[b]	1.25[a]	-34.8[a]	-3.47
	$\bar{\alpha}$	-11.2	-14.1	-131.[a]	-14.3
	$\hat{\alpha}$	28.5[a]	-0.42	-4.25[a]	0.52
$Z(t_\alpha)$	$\tilde{\alpha}$	4.51[a]	1.12[a]	-9.28[a]	-1.53
	$\bar{\alpha}$	-9.16[a]	-7.87[a]	-25.12[a]	-6.21[a]

Table V.d. Tests for Unit Roots. US.

		m	y	π	i
	τ	6.92[a]	-1.57	-1.09	-0.51
ADF	τ_μ	0.27[b]	-0.44	-1.59	-1.86
p=4	τ_τ	-2.28	-2.86	-2.00	-1.85
	τ	1.36[c]	-1.65[d]	-1.09	-4.52[a]
ADF	τ_μ	-0.99	-0.56	-1.50	-1.60
p=12	τ_τ	-3.19[d]	-3.16[d]	-1.99	-1.60
	$\hat{\alpha}$	0.19	-1.26	0.02	0.07
Z_α	$\tilde{\alpha}$	0.26[c]	0.62[b]	-0.54[d]	-2.18
	$\bar{\alpha}$	-25.0[b]	-4.29	-4.94	-9.17
	$\hat{\alpha}$	21.4[a]	-3.44[a]	0.05	0.14
$Z(t_\alpha)$	$\tilde{\alpha}$	1.77[a]	1.09[a]	-0.70	-1.29
	$\bar{\alpha}$	-16.4[a]	-2.56	-5.38[a]	-5.36[a]

Table VI. Cointegrating Regressions.

$$s = \beta_0 + \beta_1 t + \beta_2 m + \beta_3 m^* + \beta_4 y + \beta_5 y^* + \beta_6 i + \beta_7 i^* + \beta_8 \pi + \beta_9 \pi^* + u$$

	Germany / US.			Japan / US.			UK. / US.		
β_0	.	2.61	16.7	.	6.22	17.96	.	-8.54	10.22
β_1	.	.	0.02	.	.	0.01	.	.	0.02
β_2	-0.86	-1.02	-1.84	0.77	0.21	-0.32	-0.21	0.08	-1.23
β_3	0.87	0.62	-1.23	-0.58	-0.56	-1.72	-0.67	0.10	-1.11
β_4	-1.57	-1.90	-1.58	0.64	0.93	0.46	-3.37	-2.15	-0.87
β_5	-0.23	0.89	0.97	-2.69	-2.07	-1.72	5.24	1.29	1.25
β_6	0.07	-0.29	-0.77	0.70	0.48	0.20	0.68	0.10	-0.56
β_7	1.42	1.58	0.57	0.66	0.97	0.68	-4.98	-2.82	-4.35
β_8	-0.75	-0.97	0.84	1.96	-0.43	0.21	-0.94	-1.94	-1.66
β_9	-9.42	-15.43	-11.74	-4.60	-8.97	-5.94	-27.90	-8.13	-5.79
R^2	0.47	0.52	0.66	0.77	0.82	0.84	0.21	0.63	0.77
DW	0.25	0.41	0.65	0.22	0.19	0.23	0.42	0.23	0.45

Table VI.a. Residual Based Tests for Cointegration. Germany / US.

	ADF(4)	ADF(12)	Z_{α}	Z_t
Standard	-3.12	-3.11	-4.68	-2.17
Demeaned	-3.04	-2.74	-7.14	-2.94
Demeaned and Detrended	-3.61	-2.84	-17.14	-5.42

Table VI.b. Residual Based Tests for Cointegration. Japan / US.

	ADF(4)	ADF(12)	Z_{α}	Z_t
Standard	-3.03	-3.05	-6.16	-2.51
Demeaned	-3.12	-2.73	-3.67	-1.48
Demeaned and Detrended	-2.70	-2.99	-4.02	-1.63

Table VI.c. Residual Based Tests for Cointegration. UK. / US.

	ADF(4)	ADF(12)	Z_{α}	Z_t
Standard	-3.39	-3.43	-8.36	-3.15
Demeaned	-2.78	-2.59	-2.69	-1.19
Demeaned and Detrended	-3.88	-3.61	-9.49	-2.92

Chapter 4. Long Run Exchange Rate Determination II

I. Introduction

The work of Baillie and Selover (1987), Boothe and Glassman (1987) and the previous chapter takes into account the nonstationarity of some of the variables involved in the monetary models. In this context, the equations of exchange rate determination derived from the monetary models are thought of as long-run relationships. From this point of view, deviations of the exchange rate from a linear combination of its fundamentals are stationary, or in other words, they are cointegrated. The methodology used in those studies is that developed by Engle and Granger (1987). The results obtained in all three studies reject the specification of the monetary approach.

The same methodology has also been applied to a very important building block of the monetary model. The Purchasing Power Parity (PPP) as a long run equilibrium relationship has been tested by Corbae and Ouliaris (1988), Gubitz (1988), Thom (1989), Enders (1988, 1989) and Mark (1990). The evidence found in these studies is that PPP does not hold in the long run.

Using this methodology, variables that in their univariate representation have degree of integration different from unity are excluded from the cointegrating regression. On the other hand, the method used in those studies is not well designed to estimate more than one cointegrating vector.

Monetary models of exchange rate determination involve several macroeconomic variables. They are typically of different degrees of integration and possibly related by more than one cointegrating vector. Thus, both problems pointed out above are likely to appear in empirical monetary models.

In this chapter we propose a multivariate time series model which encompasses the structural monetary models. The model can be interpreted as a reduced form derived from some dynamic simultaneous equation model. On the other hand the model allows for nonstationarity and cointegration.

We use a more recent approach to cointegration that has been developed by Johansen (1988b and 1991a) and Johansen and Juselius (1990a). Using this methodology, Cheung and Lai (1990) and Johansen and Juselius (1990b) have found evidence in favor of the PPP hypothesis.

Other applications of Johansen's methodology are Baillie and Bollerslev (1989), Hall (1989), Hendry and Mizon (1989), Lee (1989) and Starck (1990).

Johansen's procedure allows for different degrees of integration and is better designed to estimate several cointegrating vectors. He derives the asymptotic distribution of the likelihood ratio tests for the number of cointegrating vectors. In addition, hypothesis tests may be conducted using standard asymptotic χ^2 tests.

We want to see if it is possible to revive the monetary model as a long run approximation in the light of these recent developments in the theory of cointegration. In this chapter we first test for the existence of cointegrating relations among the exchange rate and its fundamentals. We find several cointegrating vectors linking the exchange rate and its fundamentals. Then, we determine whether those cointegrating vectors are trivial, i.e. assign a unit coefficient to a variable that is stationary and zero to all others. We also test for a unit root in the time series defined as the difference between domestic and foreign fundamentals. If these so constructed series do not have a unit root, foreign and domestic fundamentals move together in the long run. Another hypothesis tested below is whether there is any variable that does not enter in any cointegrating vector. This is of special interest when the variable tested for is the exchange rate, since if it does not enter any of the cointegrating vectors, then they cannot be interpreted as *long run equations of exchange rate determination.* Finally, we analyze whether the cointegrating vectors have any resemblance to the *old* monetary equations described in chapter 2.

The time series model is introduced in section II. Section III describes the data set and presents diagnostic tests. Section IV analyzes the estimation and tests for cointegration. Section V tests several hypotheses. Finally, section VI concludes.

II. Description of The Time Series Model

In this section we describe the multivariate time series model that is used in the rest of the monograph. Assume that the p-dimensional time series vector X_t admits a VAR representation,

$$X_t = \Pi_1 X_{t-1} + \Pi_2 X_{t-2} + \ldots + \Pi_k X_{t-k} + \mu + \Phi D_t + \varepsilon_t, \qquad \text{(II.1)}$$

where $\varepsilon_1, \ldots, \varepsilon_T$ are $IIN(0,\Lambda)$, X_0, $X_{-1}, \ldots,$ X_{-k+1} are fixed, μ is a vector of constants and D_t are centered seasonal dummies. We will focus on the case when the matrix polynomial,

$$\Pi(z) = I - \Pi_1 z - \Pi_2 z^2 - \ldots - \Pi_k z^k \qquad \text{(II.2)}$$

is such that $|\Pi(1)|=0$, and therefore, the long run impact matrix,

$$\Pi = I - \Pi_1 - \Pi_2 - \ldots - \Pi_k, \tag{II.3}$$

has reduced rank $r<p$, where p is the number of variables in the system. This matrix can then be written as the product of two $(p\times r)$ matrices, $\Pi=\alpha\beta'$. In short, X_t is not stationary as a vector process, though we will assume that ΔX_t and the r linear combinations $\beta' X_t$ are stationary. Thus, the r columns of β are cointegrating vectors, and we will say that X_t is cointegrated with cointegrating vectors β.

The matrix β can not be uniquely estimated since it is not identified. However one can estimate a set of vectors that span the column space of β, the cointegrating space. When there is only one cointegrating vector, that linear combination of the variables is the unique stationary combination. In such a case, the cointegrating relationship is identified up to a normalization factor. When there are more than one, any linear combination of them is also stationary, and therefore there are many long run relationships that are observationally equivalent to the ones that have generated the data. Hence, the cointegrating vectors are not identified. Another way to address the issue of identification of cointegrating vectors, would be to consider $\Pi=\alpha\beta'$ as a system of equations. As long as $r>1$, we cannot uniquely recover the values of α and β from an estimate of Π.

The VAR system has an error correction representation of the form,

$$\Delta X_t = \Pi X_{t-1} + \Gamma_1 \Delta X_{t-1} + \ldots + \Gamma_{k-1} \Delta X_{t-k+1} + \mu + \Phi D_t + \varepsilon_t, \tag{II.4}$$

where $\Gamma_i = -(\Pi_{i+1} + \ldots + \Pi_k)$. One can easily see that, a VAR in first differences would suffer from misspecification unless $\Pi=0$, whereas specification of a VAR in levels would not take into account the cross equation restrictions implied by the hypothesis of cointegration, $\Pi=\alpha\beta'$.

III. The Data and Diagnostic Tests

We follow the tradition of the empirical work done on monetary models in choosing the variables that are thought of as fundamental determinants of the exchange rate. Let us stack the exchange rate and its fundamentals in a vector,

$$X_t = [s_t, m_t, m_t^*, y_t, y_t^*, i_t, i_t^*, \pi_t, \pi_t^*]',$$

where s_t is the logarithm of the spot rate, m_t is the log of the domestic money supply, y_t is the log of real national income, i_t is a money market interest rate and π_t is the expected rate of inflation over the next period. Starred variables are foreign counterparts. The choice of variables to be included in the analysis is crucial and at this point we are excluding for the analysis other variables such as cumulated trade balances, price of nontradeable and tradeable goods, etc, as possible elements of X_t. The inclusion of those would enlarge the already huge number of parameters in the model (II.1). However, one could use an alternative approach to the full system methodology as described by Johansen (1990c) or Phillips (1989). This approach requires previous knowledge about restrictions on α and the placement of unit roots in the vector X_t.

III.1. Data Description

We estimate three VAR systems for the German mark, British pound and Japanese Yen relative to the US dollar using monthly data from april 1973 to march 1986 that is described in the Data Appendix[1]. Exchange rates and money supplies (M1) are homogeneously taken from the IMF series. The money supply for the UK was corrected for the change in the accounting procedure at the beginning of 1987 before estimation[2]. National incomes have been approximated by indexes of industrial production obtained from National Government Series. The German index presented a clear outlayer in june 1984 corresponding to the strikes that took place over that month. This was also adjusted before estimation[3]. Interest rates are either money market rates or bill rates. Finally, one period ahead expected inflation rates are proxied by actual current period monthly inflation rates, i.e. $E_t\pi_{t+1} \cong \pi_t$, calculated from the consumer price indexes of the National Government Series[4].

---

1 Estimation is conditional on 12 initial observations, from april 1972 to march of 1973. Thus, we are conditioning on pre-free-floating initial conditions.

2 The difference in the definition of M1 was easily captured by a change in mean. The post january 1987 series was adjusted by $(m_{87:1}-m_{86:12})$.

3 First we run a regression of y_t on a constant term and a dummy variable 1(t=84:6) and then the estimated coefficient for that dummy variable was subtracted from the 84:6 value of y_t.

4 Previous studies use annual inflation rates as proxies for expected long run inflation. We chose monthly rather than annual rates because with annual inflation rates one cannot reduce the error term of the VAR to a white noise for any feasible lag length.

III.2. Diagnostic Tests on the Assumptions of the VAR

Two important assumptions in the model (II.1) are the independence over time and normality of the disturbance term. Below, we analyze the choice of the lag length in the VAR for the three bilateral systems testing for those assumptions.

For each system we have estimated VAR models with lags running from 1 to 14 and chose the shortest lag length k for which all equations were left with white residuals. These are k=6 for the case of Germany / US and Japan / US and k=5 for the UK / US system. Table I in Appendix A shows the Ljung-Box statistics used to test for autocorrelation. The residuals for the Germany / US system could not be reduced to white noise simultaneously for all equations at any feasible lag length. Table I includes The Ljung-Box[5] test statistic for various choices of the parameter ℓ = number of autocorrelations of the residuals included in the computations. The reason for this is that if ℓ is chosen to be small we might be ignoring correlations that arise at longer lags and if it is chosen too big then the power of the test will generally be reduced since important autocorrelations at some lags might average out with small ones at other lags.

The normality assumption is also important. Table II in Appendix A reports the Jarque and Bera test statistics for normality of the residuals from the estimated VAR systems with lag length specified above. The rèsiduals of several equations show clear departures from

---

5 $Q(\ell) = T(T+2)\sum_{\tau=1}^{\ell}(T-\tau)^{-1}r_\tau^2 \xrightarrow{d} \chi_1^2$, where r_τ^2 is the τ-lag autocorrelation.

normality in all three systems. Gonzalo (1989) has studied the small sample properties of the ML and four others estimators of cointegrating vectors under departures from normality, ARCH disturbances and misspecification of the lag length. The ML estimator does not perform worse than the others, the reason being that the ML estimator can be interpreted as a special case of multivariate least squares where the assumption of normality is not needed. The performance of the ML estimator is affected by the choice of the lag length parameter. If the estimated VAR is underparameterized the small sample bias of this estimator increases a lot with respect to the case of an overparameterized VAR. Finally, ARCH disturbances do not damage its small sample performance.

IV. Estimation And Testing For Cointegration

In order to implement Johansen's procedure it is convenient to introduce some notation. Rewrite (II.4) as,

$$H_{0t} = \alpha\beta' H_{1t} + \Gamma H_{kt} + \varepsilon_t \qquad \text{(IV.1)}$$

where $H_{0t} = \Delta X_t$, $H_{kt} = [\Delta X'_{t-1}, \Delta X'_{t-2}, \ldots, \Delta X'_{t-k+1}, D'_t, 1]'$, $H_{1t} = X_{t-1}$ and $\Gamma = [\Gamma_1, \Gamma_2, \ldots, \Gamma_{k-1}, \Phi, \mu]$. Also define the cross product matrices,

$$M_{ij} = T^{-1}\sum_{i=1}^{T} H_{it} H'_{jt}, \quad (i, j, =0, 1, k).$$

Estimation of the cointegrating space boils down to the following three steps[6]:

---

6 In chapter 7 we give a more detailed description of Johansen's

(i) Regress H_{0t} and H_{1t} on H_{kt} to obtain the residuals U_{0t} and U_{1t}. The model (V.1) can now be written as,

$$U_{0t} = \alpha\beta' U_{1t} + \varepsilon_t \tag{IV.2}$$

(ii) Form the cross products matrices, $S_{ij} = T^{-1}\sum_{t=1}^{T} U_{it}U'_{jt}$, for i,j=0,1.

(iii) Third, the ML estimator of β, $\tilde{\beta}$ is found as the r eigenvectors associated with the r largest eigenvalues that solve the characteristic equation,

$$|\lambda S_{11} - S_{10}S_{00}^{-1}S_{01}| = 0. \tag{IV.3}$$

The ML estimates of the other parameters are, $\tilde{\alpha} = S_{01}\tilde{\beta}$, $\tilde{\Lambda} = S_{00} - \tilde{\alpha}\tilde{\alpha}'$, $\tilde{\Pi} = \tilde{\alpha}\tilde{\beta}'$ and $\tilde{\Gamma} = M_{0k}M_{kk}^{-1} - \tilde{\Pi} M_{1k}M_{kk}^{-1}$.

Consider now the nested hypotheses, H_1: Π unrestricted and H_0: $\Pi = \alpha\beta'$. The likelihood ratio test statistic (trace statistic) of the hypothesis H_0 versus H_1 is $-2 \ln (L_0/L_1) = -T \sum_{i=r+1}^{p} \ln(1-\hat{\lambda}_i)$, where $\hat{\lambda}_1 > \hat{\lambda}_2 > .. > \hat{\lambda}_p$ are the eigenvalues found in (VI.3). Similarly the likelihood ratio test statistic (maximal eigenvalue statistic) of the hypothesis $H_0(r)$ that there are r cointegrating vectors against $H_0(r+1)$ that there are r+1, is given by $-2 \ln (L_{(r)}/L_{(r+1)}) = -T \ln (1-\hat{\lambda}_{r+1})$. The asymptotic distribution of these likelihood ratio test statistics is given by the trace and maximal eigenvalue of the stochastic matrix[7],

$$\int_0^1 (dU)F' \left\{\int_0^1 FF' dt\right\}^{-1} \int_0^1 F(dU') \tag{IV.4}$$

---

procedure.

7 See Johansen (1991a).

where, U(t) is a m-dimensional Brownian motion and

$$F_i(t) = \begin{cases} U_i(t) - \int_0^1 U_i(t)dt, & i = 1,\dots,m-1 \\ t - 1/2 & i = m \end{cases}$$

where m=p-r. Osterwald-Lenum (1990) has tabulated the distribution for m ≤ 11. When the Data Generating Process (DGP) has no deterministic trend but we include a constant term in the model the testing procedure is modified. Write $\mu = \alpha\beta_0'$, where β_0 is a (r×1) vector that captures nonzero means in the long run relationships. This means that μ belongs to the cointegrating space. The model with no linear trend can now be written in an error correction fashion with $\alpha\beta' X_{t-1} + \mu = \alpha\beta^{*\prime} X^*_{t-1}$ where $X^*_{t-1} = (X'_{t-1}, 1)'$ and $\beta^* = [\beta', \beta_0]'$. Using the residuals of the regressions of ΔX_t and X^*_{t-1} on $\Delta X_{t-1}, \dots, \Delta X_{t-k+1}$ and D_t, U^*_{it} i=0,1 we follow the same procedure as in (ii) and (iii) in order to obtain the eigenvalues λ^*_i. In this case, the cointegrating space has one dimension more, and this is captured by an extra row in β. The limit distribution of the trace and maximal eigenvalue statistics computed with these eigenvalues is given in Johansen (1991a) and is shown to be of the form (IV.4) with

$$F_i(t) = \begin{cases} U_i(t) & i = 1,\dots,m \\ 1 & i = m+1 \end{cases}$$

This distribution has also been tabulated by Osterwald-Lenum (1990).

We have applied this technique to the three VAR systems The trace and maximal eigenvalue statistics for the model with deterministic trend (without deterministic trend) under the sequence of null hypotheses H_1:r=0, H_2:r=1,..., H_9:r=8, (H^*_1:r=0, H^*_2:r=1,..., H^*_9:r=8) is tested up until the null hypothesis is not rejected.

The limit distributions of the trace and maximal eigenvalue

statistics for conducting inference about the cointegrating rank depends on the actual number of cointegrating relations and also on the presence of a linear trend. Johansen (1991b) shows how to proceed in making inference, this is as follows. Tables III.a and III.b of appendix A reports the trace and maximal eigenvalue statistics respectively. Going from bottom to top of the tables we stop when the null hypothesis $H_0(r)$ is not rejected. If $H_0^*(r)$ ($\subset H_0(r)$) is rejected the presence of a linear trend is accepted.

Using this criterion and a 5% significance critical region, the Germany / US system has three cointegrating vectors and a linear trend. Inference is more difficult in the case of the Japan / US and UK / US systems because the trace and maximal eigenvalue statistics give different answers. According to the trace statistic the Japan / US system has six cointegrating vectors and a linear trend, whereas based on the maximal eigenvalue statistic it has five cointegrating vectors and no linear trend. Finally, the UK / US system has r=4 according to the trace statistic and r=1 according to the maximal eigenvalue and in both cases a linear trend.

Let $V = (v_1, \ldots, v_p)$ be the p eigenvectors resulting from (IV.3). Not all of them are cointegrating vectors. Only those associated with the r largest eigenvalues, are such that $v_i'X_t$ is a stationary variable. The choice of the number of cointegrating vectors is difficult since the maximal eigenvalue and trace tests give different answers in general. Following Johansen and Juselius (1990a) we now look at the graphs of $v_i'X_t$. By observing those graphs, we may be able to tell whether a given combination $v_i'X_t$ is stationary. In appendix B we show the graphs of $v_i'X_t$, $i = 1, \ldots, 9$ for all three VAR systems.

The Germany / US case presents graphs of cointegrating

residuals $v_i'X_t$ for $i = 1$ to 3, that appear to be stationary, the remaining graphs capture nonstationary components, thus we choose $r = 3$. The first five graphs of the Japan / US system seem to be stationary. The graph of the sixth cointegrating residual may also be considered as stationary though this is arguable since it presents a change in mean during the period mid-74 to 76. The choice here is limited between five and six cointegrating vectors. The analysis that follows assumes $r = 6$. Finally, the British-American case looks like there are four stationary cointegrating residuals even though the stationarity of the third one can be questioned. Here we have chosen to take $r = 4$.

Table V reports the estimated cointegrating vectors for the three systems. It is difficult to interpret those numerical values given the problem of identification commented above.

In the following sections we will proceed to test several hypotheses on those cointegrating vectors as well as on the constant term μ and the loadings matrix α.

V. Tests of Several Hypotheses

V.1. Testing for Known Cointegrating Vectors

We follow Johansen and Juselius (1990a) in implementing the likelihood ratio test statistic for testing this type of hypothesis. Suppose we want to test the hypothesis $\beta = (G,\psi)$ where G is a known $(p\times r_1)$ matrix and ψ is a $(p\times r_2)$ unknown matrix of cointegrating vectors, with $r = r_1 + r_2$. Accordingly, split α as (α_1,α_2) and rewrite model (IV.2) as,

$$U_{0t} = \alpha_1 G' U_{1t} + \alpha_2 \psi' U_{1t} + \varepsilon_t. \qquad \text{(V.1)}$$

Further concentrating the model by regressing U_{0t} and U_{1t} on $G'U_{1t}$ obtaining the new residuals U_{0Gt} and U_{1Gt} respectively gives,

$$U_{0Gt} = \alpha_2 \psi' U_{1Gt} + \varepsilon_t. \qquad \text{(V.2)}$$

Equation (V.2) is a reduced rank regression model. Johansen and Juselius (1990a) show how the estimation of ψ requires to solve the following series of eigenvalue problems. First define the cross product matrices,

$$S_{kjG} = T^{-1} \sum_{t=1}^{T} U_{kGt} U'_{jGt} \qquad k, j = 0, 1,$$

solve the eigenvalue problem,

$$|\rho I - S_{11G}| = 0,$$

and construct $C = (u_1, \ldots, u_{p-r_1}) \operatorname{diag}(\rho_1^{-1/2}, \ldots, \rho_{p-r_1}^{-1/2})$ from the $(p-r_1)$ eigenvectors associated with the $(p-r_1)$ greatest eigenvalues. Then, solve the eigenvalue problem,

$$|\eta I - C' S_{10G} S_{00G}^{-1} S_{01G} C| = 0. \qquad \text{(V.3)}$$

The maximum likelihood estimate of ψ are given by C times the r_2 eigenvectors $(v_1, \ldots, v_{r_2})$ associated with the r_2 largest eigenvalues $\eta_1 > \ldots > \eta_{r_2} > 0$. Therefore the matrix of cointegrating vectors is $\beta = (G, C(v_1, \ldots, v_{r_2}))$.

The derivation of the likelihood ratio test statistic of the null hypothesis H_0: $\beta = (G, \psi)$ against the alternative H_1: β unspecified, requires to solve an additional eigenvalue problem given by,

$$|\delta G'S_{11}G - G'S_{10}S_{00}^{-1}S_{01}G| = 0. \qquad (V.4)$$

The likelihood ratio statistic is given by,

$$-2\log(L(H_1)/L(H_0)) = T\ \{\sum_{i=1}^{r_1}\ln(1-\delta_i) + \sum_{i=1}^{r_2}\ln(1-\eta_i) - \sum_{i=1}^{r}\ln(1-\lambda_i)\},$$

where δ_i, η_i and λ_i are the eigenvalues associated with (V.4), (V.3) and (IV.3) respectively. It has a χ^2 asymptotic distribution with $(p-r)r_1$ degrees of freedom.

V.1.1 Testing for Trivial Cointegrating Vectors

Some of the exchange rate fundamentals have been found to be stationary processes when a unit root test in their univariate representation was performed. Previous analysis of monetary models of exchange rate determination using cointegration theory have found evidence in this direction[8]. In chapter 3 we have analyzed the existence of unit roots in the univariate representation of the variables used in this chapter, finding no unit roots in some of the series.

Johansen's definition of cointegration allows for some of the individual variables to be stationary. It only requires the vector time series X_t to be nonstationary as a vector process[9]. Trivial cointegrating vectors may now appear, since one can always form a linear

---

8 Baillie and Selover (1987) and Boothe and Glassman (1987).

9 Note that the nonstationarity of a multivariate time series does not imply that each of its univariate components should be nonstationary.

combination of a stationary variable and a nonstationary one that assigns a unit coefficient to the former and a zero coefficient to the latter. This gives more flexibility to the analysis as commented by Johansen (1988a).

It is interesting to test for the possible existence of those trivial cointegrating vectors. If there were only trivial cointegrating vectors, we could not argue that the exchange rate and the other variables are linked by long run relationships.

Suppose we want to test whether there is a cointegrating vector that assigns a unit coefficient to the i-th variable and zero to all the rest. The matrix of cointegrating vectors can be expressed as, $\beta = (e_i, \psi)$ where e_i is the i-th unit vector and ψ is a $(p\times(r-1))$ matrix of cointegrating vectors. The construction of the likelihood ratio test follows the procedure described at the beginning of this section.

Table VIII.a reports the values of those test statistics for trivial cointegrating vectors. The German / US system presents no trivial cointegrating vectors. On the other hand, we accept the null for the cases of Japanese and British interest and inflation rates. The value of the statistic for British and Japanese inflations are close to the critical value at the 5% significance level. When the two trivial cointegrating vectors are jointly tested for, we accept the joint hypothesis for both systems (see table VIII.b).

Summarizing, the Germany / US system does not present trivial cointegrating vectors. The Japan / US system has two of them, corresponding to the Japanese interest and inflation rates. Finally, the UK / US system has also two trivial cointegrating vector associated with the British interest and inflation rates.

V.1.2. Testing for Cointegration between Fundamentals

In this section we test for the existence of cointegrating relationships between pairs of foreign and domestic fundamentals of the form:

H_1: $\beta = (b_1,\psi)$, where $b_1 = (0,1,-1,0,0,0,0,0,0)'$

H_2: $\beta = (b_2,\psi)$, where $b_2 = (0,0,0,1,-1,0,0,0,0)'$

H_3: $\beta = (b_3,\psi)$, where $b_3 = (0,0,0,0,0,1,-1,0,0)'$

H_4: $\beta = (b_4,\psi)$, where $b_4 = (0,0,0,0,0,0,0,1,-1)'$.

The hypothesis H_1 means that the logarithm of the money supplies ratio is stationary by itself. Similarly, H_2 assumes the logarithm of the domestic to foreign national income ratio is stationary. The same is implied in H_3 and H_4 for the interest and inflation differentials respectively. If these hypotheses are true, there are long run relationships that keep domestic and foreign fundamentals at a constant difference so deviations from that level are temporary.

The testing procedure is the same as the one explained in section V.2. We have calculated the likelihood ratio statistics to individually test those hypotheses for the three systems, and we have collected them in table VIII.c. Only the inflation differentials in the UK / US system is stationary at the 5 % level of significance, though the hypothesis is rejected at the 10 % level.

The inflation differential is stationary in the UK / US system and let us suppose that we can interpret this as a cointegrating vector. If this cointegrating vector enters the pound / dollar rate equation of the ECM with a nonzero coefficient, then the pound dollar rate would increase any time that the British inflation is greater than the US inflation and viceversa. This relationship between the change in the pound / dollar rate and the UK / US inflation differential can be viewed as a reflection of *ex-post relative purchasing power parity.*

In addition, we also test for the joint hypothesis of stationarity of the British interest rate, inflation rate and the symmetry between the inflation rates in the UK / US system. This amounts to imposing two known cointegrating vectors in the UK / US system of the form, $\beta = (G,\psi)$ where $G = (e_6, e_8, b_4)$. Even though both hypotheses are accepted individually, they are rejected when jointly considered, see table VIII.d. In what follows we will only impose the trivial cointegrating vectors in the UK / US system.

V.2. Tests of the same Linear Restrictions on all Cointegrating Vectors

These restrictions can be written in matrix form as $\beta = J\,\varphi$, where J is a (p×s) matrix of constants and φ is a (s×r) matrix of unknown coefficients. If $\beta' X_t$ is a stationary r-dimensional process then, these restrictions imply that $\varphi' J' X_t = \varphi' Y_t$ is a stationary s-dimensional vector. Thus the cointegration space lies in the subspace spanned by the columns of φ. In order to carry out a formal test of this hypothesis, the restricted cointegration space is estimated as the r eigenvectors associated with the r largest eigenvalues of the characteristic equation,

$$|\lambda\, J'S_{11}J - J'S_{10}S_{00}^{-1}S_{01}J| = 0. \qquad \text{(V.5)}$$

The likelihood ratio test of the null hypothesis $H_0 : \beta = J\varphi$ against the alternative $H_1 :\ \Pi = \alpha\beta'$ is given by, $T\sum_{i=1}^{r} \ln\{(1-\hat{\lambda}_{0i})/(1-\hat{\lambda}_{1i})\}$, where $\hat{\lambda}_{0i}$

and $\hat{\lambda}_{1i}$ are the eigenvalues under the null and alternative hypotheses respectively. The asymptotic distribution of this likelihood ratio test statistic is shown by Johansen (1991a) to be χ^2 with r(p-s) degrees of freedom.

V.2.1. Testing the Exclusion of a Variable from all Cointegrating Vectors

We now turn to testing for the exclusion of a variable from all the cointegrating vectors. The interest of such a test is that if a variable is absent from all long run relationships, the long run behavior of the system does not depend on that variable. This, however, does not imply that the dynamics of that variable are not affected by the deviations from the long run relationships. We will test for the effects of the cointegrating residuals on the dynamics of the variables in the following chapter.

In terms of exchange rate determination the type of tests analyzed in this section have a special meaning. If the exchange rate is excluded from all the cointegrating vectors, the long run monetary equations of exchange rate determination *a la* Frankel (1979, 1984) would not make much sense, since the exchange rate is excluded from all long run equilibrium relationships.

For the purpose of testing for the absence of the i-th variable from all the cointegrating vectors the matrix J would take the form of a (9x9) identity matrix with the i-th column deleted. If the variable tested for exclusion was the exchange rate, J would be,

$$J = \begin{bmatrix} 0 & 0 & 0 & 0 & 0 & 0 & 0 & 0 \\ 1 & 0 & 0 & 0 & 0 & 0 & 0 & 0 \\ 0 & 1 & 0 & 0 & 0 & 0 & 0 & 0 \\ 0 & 0 & 1 & 0 & 0 & 0 & 0 & 0 \\ 0 & 0 & 0 & 1 & 0 & 0 & 0 & 0 \\ 0 & 0 & 0 & 0 & 1 & 0 & 0 & 0 \\ 0 & 0 & 0 & 0 & 0 & 1 & 0 & 0 \\ 0 & 0 & 0 & 0 & 0 & 0 & 1 & 0 \\ 0 & 0 & 0 & 0 & 0 & 0 & 0 & 1 \end{bmatrix}$$

The empirical application of these tests to the three bilateral systems gave the results summarized in table IX. None of the variables could be excluded from all the cointegrating vectors, meaning that all play some role in the long run relations characterizing the dynamics of the systems. For the Japan / US and UK / US systems we already know that the British and Japanese interest and inflation rates enter in some cointegrating vector, at least trivially. Therefore, the exclusion of these variables from all cointegrating vectors is not accepted.

V.2.2. Testing for the Restrictions of a Monetary Equation

Do the non trivial cointegrating vectors that we have found reflect the restrictions given by the monetary equation (3.III.1)?. In order to answer this question we will test for the same restrictions in all nontrivial cointegrating vectors. The analysis in this section is divided in two parts. The first part deals with the Germany / US system where there are no trivial cointegrating vectors. The second treats the other two systems where we found various trivial cointegrating vectors.

In the case of Germany, we proceed by testing for the equality of the coefficients in absolute terms, first of those associated with the money supplies, then outputs, interest rates, and finally inflation rates. The testing procedure follows the same steps outlined in section V.2.

If $X_t = [s_t, m_t, m^*_t, y_t, y^*_t, i_t, i^*_t, \pi_t, \pi^*_t]'$ and the i-th column of β is denoted by $\beta'_i = [\beta_{i1}, \beta_{i2}, \beta_{i3}, \beta_{i4}, \beta_{i5}, \beta_{i6}, \beta_{i7}, \beta_{i8}, \beta_{i9}]$ for i = 1,..,r, then p = 9, s = 8 and the hypotheses are written as,

$$H^1_0: \beta_{i2} = -\beta_{i3}, \quad i = 1,\dots,r$$
$$H^2_0: \beta_{i4} = -\beta_{i5}, \quad i = 1,\dots,r$$
$$H^3_0: \beta_{i6} = -\beta_{i7}, \quad i = 1,\dots,r$$
$$H^4_0: \beta_{i8} = -\beta_{i9}, \quad i = 1,\dots,r.$$

The J matrices associated with these hypotheses are,

$$J_1 = \begin{bmatrix} 1&0&0&0&0&0&0&0 \\ 0&1&0&0&0&0&0&0 \\ 0&-1&0&0&0&0&0&0 \\ 0&0&1&0&0&0&0&0 \\ 0&0&0&1&0&0&0&0 \\ 0&0&0&0&1&0&0&0 \\ 0&0&0&0&0&1&0&0 \\ 0&0&0&0&0&0&1&0 \\ 0&0&0&0&0&0&0&1 \end{bmatrix} \qquad J_2 = \begin{bmatrix} 1&0&0&0&0&0&0&0 \\ 0&1&0&0&0&0&0&0 \\ 0&0&1&0&0&0&0&0 \\ 0&0&0&1&0&0&0&0 \\ 0&0&0&-1&0&0&0&0 \\ 0&0&0&0&1&0&0&0 \\ 0&0&0&0&0&1&0&0 \\ 0&0&0&0&0&0&1&0 \\ 0&0&0&0&0&0&0&1 \end{bmatrix}$$

$$J_3 = \begin{bmatrix} 1&0&0&0&0&0&0&0 \\ 0&1&0&0&0&0&0&0 \\ 0&0&1&0&0&0&0&0 \\ 0&0&0&1&0&0&0&0 \\ 0&0&0&0&1&0&0&0 \\ 0&0&0&0&0&1&0&0 \\ 0&0&0&0&0&-1&0&0 \\ 0&0&0&0&0&0&1&0 \\ 0&0&0&0&0&0&0&1 \end{bmatrix} \qquad J_4 = \begin{bmatrix} 1&0&0&0&0&0&0&0 \\ 0&1&0&0&0&0&0&0 \\ 0&0&1&0&0&0&0&0 \\ 0&0&0&1&0&0&0&0 \\ 0&0&0&0&1&0&0&0 \\ 0&0&0&0&0&1&0&0 \\ 0&0&0&0&0&0&1&0 \\ 0&0&0&0&0&0&0&1 \\ 0&0&0&0&0&0&0&-1 \end{bmatrix}$$

None of the hypotheses H^1_0, H^2_0, H^3_0 and H^4_0 is accepted for the German case. The test statistics are reported in table X of Appendix A.

For the other two systems, the existence of trivial cointegrating vectors makes it necessary to modify the testing procedure used above. We will test the null hypothesis $\beta=(G, J_i\varphi)$ where G is a (9×2) matrix of trivial cointegrating vectors, J_i is any of the (9×8) matrices $J_1,..,J_4$ defined above and φ is an unknown $(8\times r_2)$ matrix where $r_2 = r-2$. The alternative is defined as $\beta=(G,\psi)$ where ψ is an unknown $(9\times r_2)$ matrix.

Using equation (V.2), substituting $\psi = J\varphi$ gives,

$$U_{0Gt} = \alpha_2 \varphi' J' \; U_{1Gt} + \varepsilon_t . \qquad \text{(V.6)}$$

Now, we are in the set up of section V.2, so we have to solve the eigenvalue problem,

$$|\lambda J_1' S_{11G} J_1 - J_1' S_{10G} S_{00G}^{-1} S_{01G} J_1| = 0. \qquad \text{(V.7)}$$

The likelihood ratio test is given by,

$$-2\log(L(H_1)/L(H_0)) = T \; \{ \sum_{i=1}^{r_2} \ln(1-\eta_i) \; - \; \sum_{i=1}^{r_2} \ln(1-\lambda_i)\},$$

where η_i and λ_i are the r_2 largest eigenvalues associated with (V.?) and (V.7) respectively. This likelihood ratio statistic is asymptotically distributed as a χ^2 with r_2 degrees of freedom.

Table X reports the test statistics of these hypotheses for the Japan / US and UK / US systems. Only the symmetry between the money supplies of the US and the UK is accepted.

This symmetry between US and UK money supplies can be interpreted as saying that the long run effect of an increase in the British money supply by 1 pound is equivalent to a drop in the US money supply by 1 dollar. Note, however, that we are not imposing the restriction that the coefficient assigned to $(m-m^*)$ in the cointegrating vectors of the UK / US system must be equal to one, which is usual practice in theoretical monetary models.

VI. Conclusions

In this chapter we have found several cointegrating vectors linking three main dollar exchange rates with macroeconomic fundamentals. Some of the cointegrating vectors, but not all, were found to be trivial, meaning that the nontrivial ones can be interpreted as equations of long run exchange rate determination. None of the variables was excluded from all cointegrating vectors. This is important because if the exchange rate was excluded from all cointegrating vectors, then none of them could be interpreted as a long run exchange rate equation. Finally, the cointegrating vectors do not satisfy the restrictions imposed by the *old* monetary equations.

If the cointegrating vectors are interpreted as long run exchange rate equations they would measure how the exchange rate reacts in the long run to permanent changes in its fundamentals.

Up to now we have tested several restrictions on the matrix of cointegrating vectors β. In the next chapter we test restrictions on the loadings matrix α. This matrix measures the weights with which the error correction term enters each equation of the ECM. That is, how the exchange rate reacts in the short run to transitory deviations of the fundamentals from their long run values.

APPENDIX A

Table I. Ljung - Box Statistics for l = 12, 24, 36.

	Germany / US		Japan / US		UK /US	
	Q(12)= 18.82	.92E-01	Q(12)= 5.507	.93	Q(12)= 9.783	.63
s	Q(24)= 28.21	.25	Q(24)= 29.17	.21	Q(24)= 21.32	.61
	Q(36)= 34.72	.52	Q(36)= 42.84	.20	Q(36)= 30.39	.73
	Q(12)= 12.86	.37	Q(12)= 18.49	.10	Q(12)= 10.14	.60
m	Q(24)= 20.41	.67	Q(24)= 30.79	.15	Q(24)= 19.50	.72
	Q(36)= 35.22	.50	Q(36)= 43.72	.17	Q(36)= 26.31	.88
	Q(12)= 5.879	.92	Q(12)= 10.32	.58	Q(12)= 13.12	.35
m^*	Q(24)= 15.42	.90	Q(24)= 19.12	.74	Q(24)= 23.13	.51
	Q(36)= 21.13	.97	Q(36)= 32.41	.63	Q(36)= 44.66	.15
	Q(12)= 6.378	.89	Q(12)= 8.590	.73	Q(12)= 9.434	.66
y	Q(24)= 25.73	.36	Q(24)= 30.60	.16	Q(24)= 21.41	.61
	Q(36)= 38.34	.36	Q(36)= 47.69	.91E-01	Q(36)= 26.70	.86
	Q(12)= 6.275	.90	Q(12)= 13.33	.34	Q(12)= 3.920	.98
y^*	Q(24)= 32.48	.11	Q(24)= 25.29	.39	Q(24)= 21.16	.62
	Q(36)= 40.53	.27	Q(36)= 28.05	.82	Q(36)= 28.38	.81
	Q(12)= 32.73	.10E-02	Q(12)= 13.67	.32	Q(12)= 12.02	.44
i	Q(24)= 48.04	.24E-02	Q(24)= 24.78	.41	Q(24)= 22.34	.55
	Q(36)= 57.20	.13E-01	Q(36)= 36.74	.43	Q(36)= 31.68	.67
	Q(12)= 11.25	.50	Q(12)= 12.19	.43	Q(12)= 16.58	.16
i^*	Q(24)= 30.49	.16	Q(24)= 26.57	.32	Q(24)= 27.46	.28
	Q(36)= 45.69	.12	Q(36)= 31.95	.66	Q(36)= 40.09	.29
	Q(12)= 12.47	.40	Q(12)= 10.20	.59	Q(12)= 7.514	.82
π	Q(24)= 22.21	.56	Q(24)= 21.31	.61	Q(24)= 21.77	.59
	Q(36)= 38.14	.37	Q(36)= 28.92	.79	Q(36)= 33.94	.56
	Q(12)= 11.72	.46	Q(12)= 7.223	.84	Q(12)= 17.06	.14
π^*	Q(24)= 19.08	.74	Q(24)= 18.72	.76	Q(24)= 32.05	.12
	Q(36)= 31.55	.67	Q(36)= 33.60	.58	Q(36)= 43.69	.17

p values to the right.

Table II. Jarque and Bera Tests for Normality.

	Germany / US	
s	J&B(2) = 7.99	.02
m_*	J&B(2) = 11.0	.39E-02
m	J&B(2) = 2.32	.31
y_*	J&B(2) = 1.30	.52
y	J&B(2) = 6.35	.41E-01
i_*	J&B(2) = 0.84	.65
i	J&B(2) = 0.95	.62
π_*	J&B(2) = 9.36	.92E-02
π	J&B(2) = 22.3	.00

p values to the right.

	Japan / US	
s	J&B(2) = 20.6	.32E-04
m_*	J&B(2) = 10.0	.65E-02
m	J&B(2) = 0.67	.71
y_*	J&B(2) = 1.14	.56
y	J&B(2) = 3.25	.19
i_*	J&B(2) = 9.50	.86E-02
i	J&B(2) = 2.98	.22
π_*	J&B(2) = 36.4	.00
π	J&B(2) = 46.8	.00

p values to the right.

	UK / US	
s	J&B(2) = 10.7	.46E-02
m_*	J&B(2) = 6.85	.32E-01
m	J&B(2) = 0.04	.97
y_*	J&B(2) = 54.4	.00
y	J&B(2) = 2.59	.27
i_*	J&B(2) = 21.8	.17E-04
i	J&B(2) = 4.64	.98E-01
π_*	J&B(2) = 910.	.00
π	J&B(2) = 15.0	.55E-03

p values to the right.

Table III Tests for Cointegration

Trace Statistic.

	Germany / US		Japan / US		UK / US	
	H_0	H_0^*	H_0	H_0^*	H_0	H_0^*
r = 8	2.50	6.41	1.03	9.61[c]	2.25	4.10
r = 7	12.12	17.20	12.53	22.43[b]	9.71	13.30
r = 6	24.50	29.59	28.05[d]	40.99[b]	26.69	30.29
r = 5	39.84	48.01	50.23[c]	63.18[a]	45.60[d]	49.90[d]
r = 4	60.28	70.93	87.85[a]	104.19[a]	66.89[d]	77.26[c]
r = 3	87.26	111.41[a]	130.86[a]	154.40[a]	94.54[c]	107.48[b]
r = 2	133.06[b]	163.99[a]	181.81[a]	218.73[a]	128.81[b]	151.92[a]
r = 1	191.02[a]	228.94[a]	249.05[a]	287.83[a]	180.14[a]	224.30[a]
r = 0	257.05[a]	311.47[a]	321.48[a]	376.12[a]	262.76[a]	309.19[a]

a significant at the 1 %　　c significant at the 5%
b significant at the 2.5 %　　d significant at the 10%

Table III Tests for Cointegration.

Maximal Eigenvalue Statistic.

	Germany / US		Japan / US		UK / US	
H_0	H_0	H_0^*	H_0	H_0^*	H_0	H_0^*
r = 8	2.50	6.41	1.03	9.61[c]	2.25	4.10
r = 7	9.62	10.80	11.50	12.82	7.46	9.20
r = 6	12.37	12.38	15.52	18.56	16.98	16.99
r = 5	15.35	18.43	22.18	22.19	18.91	19.61
r = 4	20.44	22.92	37.61[b]	41.01[a]	21.28	27.35
r = 3	26.97	40.48[c]	43.01[b]	50.20[a]	27.65	30.23
r = 2	45.80[c]	52.58[a]	50.95[b]	64.34[a]	34.27	44.43[d]
r = 1	57.96[a]	64.94[a]	67.24[a]	69.09[a]	51.33[d]	72.38[a]
r = 0	66.02[a]	82.53[a]	72.42[a]	88.30[a]	82.61[a]	84.89[a]

a significant at the 1 %　　c significant at the 5%
b significant at the 2.5 %　　d significant at the 10%

Table IV. Cointegrating Vectors.

Germany / US.

s	m	m^*	y	y^*	i	i^*	π	π^*
-7.74	-8.16	4.11	-47.93	19.82	55.95	-37.6	-1340.7	174.54
-10.94	-42.97	21.94	42.19	-3.46	-184.35	153.91	411.56	-914.56
11.33	-5.7	-2.36	48.88	-34.22	-67.52	159.69	-1053.3	83.00

Japan / US.

s	m	m^*	y	y^*	i	i^*	π	π^*
6.55	10.21	-9.74	49.92	-47.8	-9.77	-53.87	-211.11	791.8
-2.26	-0.81	-15.35	-2.91	26.6	89.3	13.46	-490.56	-637.14
15.1	-1.18	19.37	-69.01	51.88	2.51	106.89	133.05	-395.11
6.54	-14.16	12.55	1.73	-10.04	-83.02	16.64	-266.17	454.45
10.49	-14.41	8.55	-15.31	28.13	18.74	35.04	-234.35	396.1
9.02	9.84	-22.27	3.04	39.19	15.17	6.11	57.81	-335.82

UK / US.

s	m	m^*	y	y^*	i	i^*	π	π^*
7.67	-6.46	10.52	6.47	-12.44	39.53	-15.25	-321.43	818.48
1.05	7.69	-2.13	-39.24	-9.3	-16.16	-42.66	-117.6	482.08
11.28	-3.27	0.62	2.07	-17.44	30.27	65.76	23.91	-137.59
-7.83	-7.37	19.41	-36.07	19.76	-13.38	-45.08	170.91	230.4

Table V. Tests for Trivial Cointegrating Vectors.

	Germany / US.	Japan / US.	UK / US.
s	33.379[a]	8.264[c]	13.207[b]
m_*	29.517[a]	9.203[c]	12.092[b]
m	32.593[a]	14.924[a]	12.794[b]
y_*	31.409[a]	13.591[a]	11.163[c]
y	33.655[a]	10.633[b]	14.773[b]
i_*	29.416[a]	1.679	4.591
i	24.011[a]	10.807[b]	12.978[b]
π_*	31.198[a]	6.830[d]	10.140[d]
π	30.099[a]	13.536[a]	13.230[b]
	$\chi^2_{(6)}$	$\chi^2_{(3)}$	$\chi^2_{(5)}$

Table VI. Joint Tests for Various Trivial Cointegrating Vectors.

	Japan / US.	UK / US.
i and π	8.002	14.108
	$\chi^2_{(6)}$	$\chi^2_{(10)}$

Table VII. Tests of Cointegration Between Fundamentals.

	Germany / US.	Japan / US.	UK / US.
$m - m^*$	38.851[a]	16.276[a]	11.455[c]
$y - y^*$	34.639[a]	12.523[a]	15.565[a]
$i - i^*$	31.085[a]	9.8632[b]	20.439[a]
$\pi - \pi^*$	30.995[a]	7.8813[c]	9.8485[d]
	$\chi^2_{(6)}$	$\chi^2_{(3)}$	$\chi^2_{(5)}$

Table VIII. Joint Tests of Trivial Cointegrating Vectors

and Cointegration Between Fundamentals.

	UK / US.
i, π and $\pi - \pi^*$	55.373[a]
	$\chi^2_{(15)}$

Table IX. Tests for the Absence of a Variable from all Cointegrating Vectors.

	Germany / US.	Japan / US.	UK / US
s	15.607[a]	26.041[a]	32.197[a]
m_*	23.640[a]	27.789[a]	22.539[a]
m	10.810[b]	27.952[a]	10.859[c]
y_*	22.572[a]	39.636[a]	27.031[a]
y	15.952[a]	34.639[a]	19.177[a]
i_*	29.446[a]	38.236[a]	26.948[a]
i	24.547[a]	36.328[a]	12.139[b]
π_*	31.409[a]	43.651[a]	43.690[a]
π	21.453[a]	43.729[a]	38.602[a]
	$\chi^2_{(3)}$	$\chi^2_{(6)}$	$\chi^2_{(4)}$

Table X. Tests for the same restrictions in all non-trivial Cointegrating Vectors.

	Germany / US.	Japan / US.	UK / US.
$m - m_*$	33.463[a]	28.696[a]	2.3618
$y - y_*$	24.096[a]	15.940[a]	32.771[a]
$i - i_*$	25.493[a]	37.995[a]	26.917[a]
$\pi - \pi_*$	32.203[a]	37.995[a]	26.917[a]
	$\chi^2_{(3)}$	$\chi^2_{(4)}$	$\chi^2_{(2)}$

APPENDIX B

In this appendix we have collected all graphs of the time series defined as $v_i'X_t$ for i = 1,...,9 where v_i is the i-th eigenvector of (VI.3). We will call these series cointegrating residuals though for i = r+1,....,9 this terminology is incorrect.

Figure I. Cointegrating residuals, Germany / US.

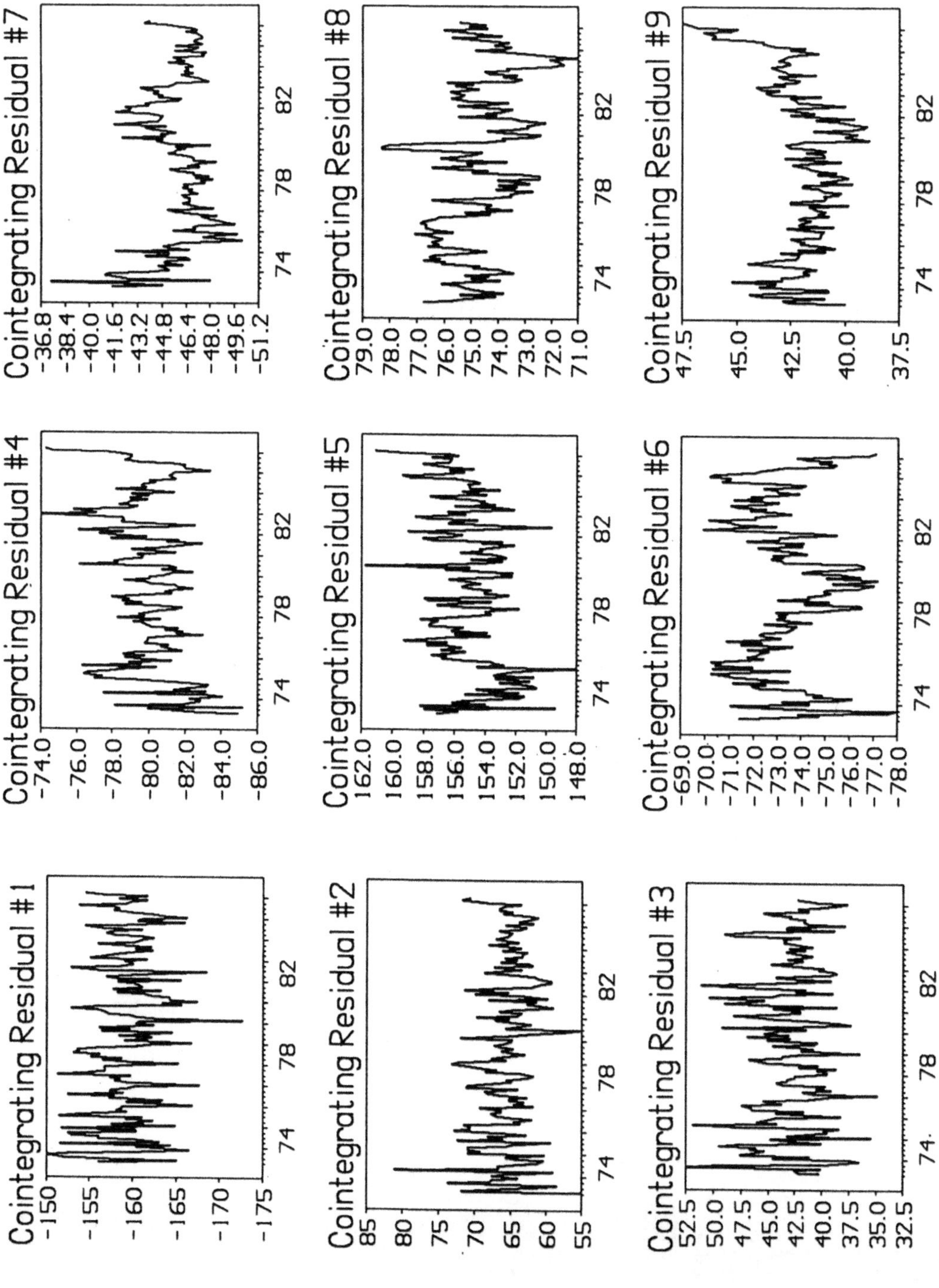

Figure II. Cointegrating residuals, Japan / US.

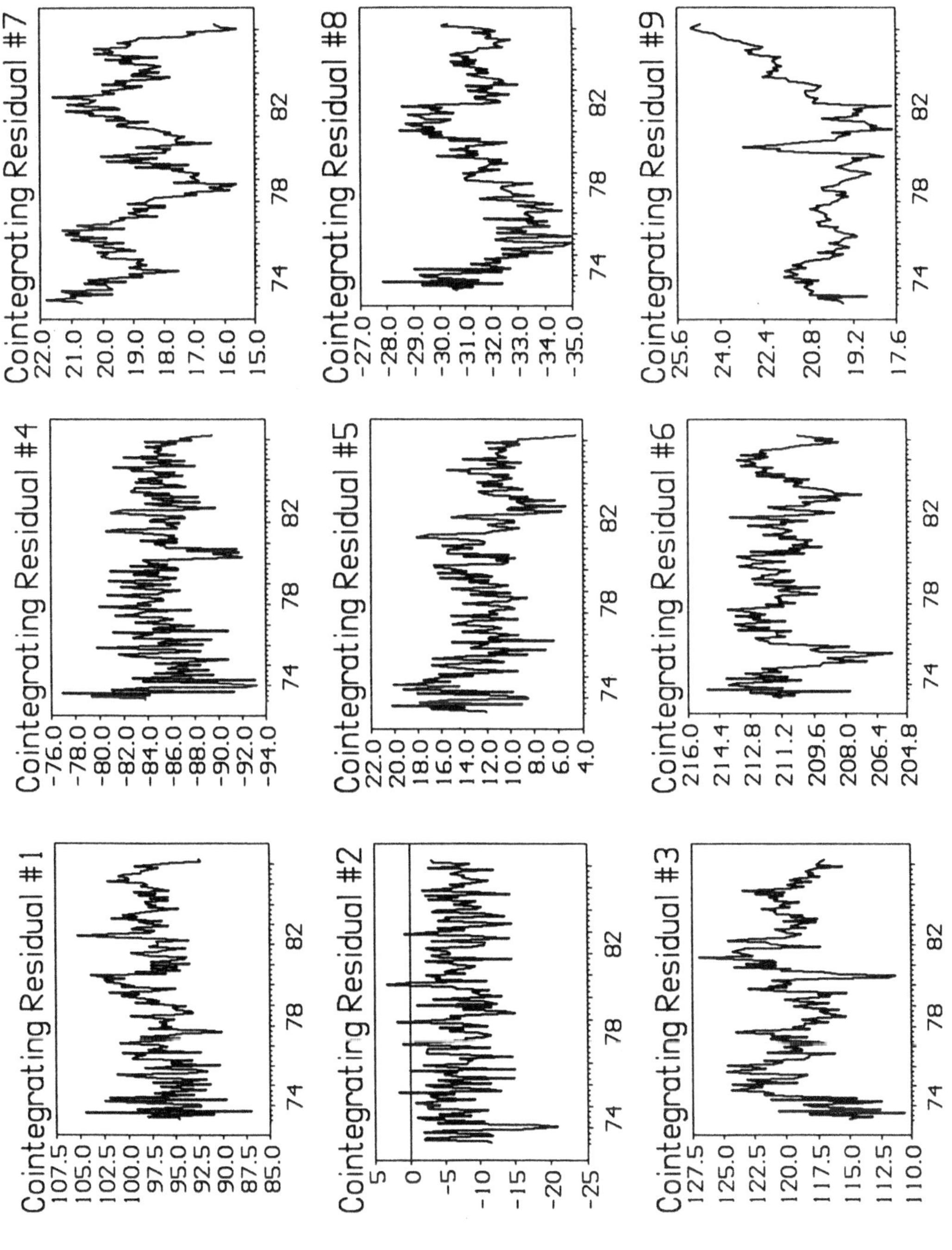

Figure III. Cointegrating residuals, UK / US.

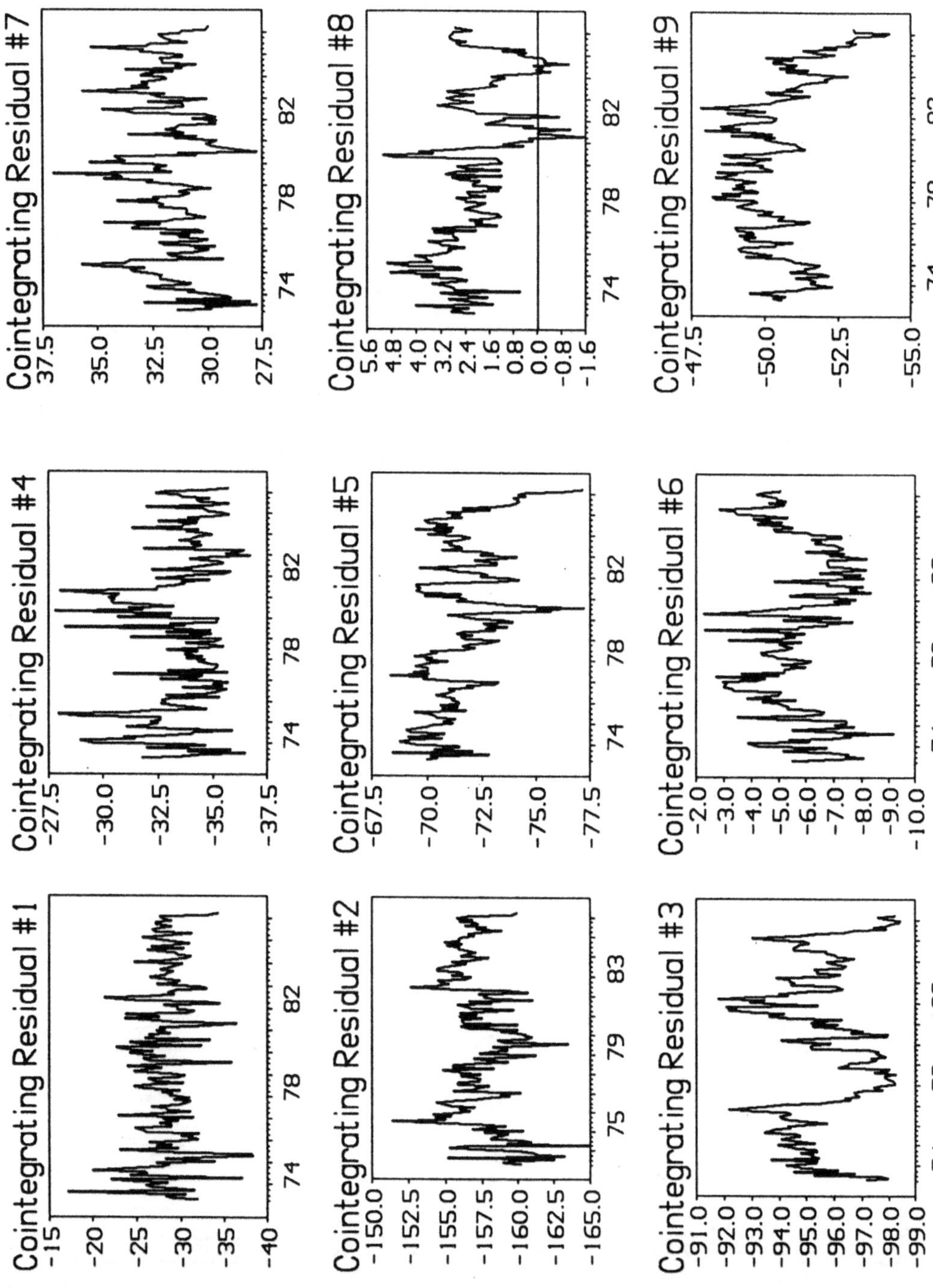

Chapter 5. Short Run Exchange Rate Determination

I. Introduction

In this chapter we study the short run dynamics of the exchange rate. In particular, we are interested in how the exchange rate reacts to transitory deviations from the long run equilibrium. By inspecting the ECM we can see that the loadings matrix α plays an extremely important role in this matter.

The implications of weak exogeneity of a variable with respect to the cointegrating vectors are analyzed in section II. In section III we follow Johansen and Juselius (1990a) and Johansen (1991a) in deriving a test for weak exogeneity. In the empirical application we find the exchange rates studied to be weakly exogenous with respect to the cointegrating vectors. Section IV shows how one can derive the asset market model of exchange rate determination from an ECM. A necessary condition is that the exchange rate cannot be weakly exogenous with respect to the cointegrating vectors. This is precisely the opposite from what we obtain.

II. Weak Exogeneity of the Exchange Rate

The short run dynamics of the exchange rate and all the other variables in the system are determined by the ECM (4.II.4) reproduced below,

$$\Delta X_t = \alpha\beta' X_{t-1} + \Gamma_1 \Delta X_{t-1} + \ldots + \Gamma_{k-1} \Delta X_{t-k+1} + \mu + \Phi D_t + \varepsilon_t . \qquad \text{(II.1)}$$

It specifies how the variables change over time as a function of four components:

a) The deviations to the r long run equilibrium relationships.

b) Past changes in all variables.

c) A purely deterministic component (constant term plus seasonal dummies).

d) A stochastic disturbance.

The first component deserves a little more attention than the rest. The loadings matrix α, measures how the different variables in the system react to the stationary equilibrium errors $\beta' X_t = Y_t$. Consider the error correction model (II.1) and rewrite it as,

$$\Delta X_t = \alpha Y_{t-1} + \sum_{i=1}^{k-1} \Gamma_i \Delta X_{t-i} + \mu + \Phi D_t + \varepsilon_t . \qquad \text{(II.2)}$$

A generic element of this matrix, α_{ij} measures the force of adjustment with which the i-th variable of the system reacts to deviations from the j-th long-run relationship.

If $\alpha_{ij} = 0$ for $j=1,..,r$, then the i-th variable can be considered as weakly exogenous with respect to the parameters of interest β, so that the estimation of β can be performed conditional on the i-th variable, thus, reducing by one the dimension of the system.

In order to perform the exogeneity tests it is convenient to write the joint hypothesis $H_0 : \alpha_{ij} = 0$ for $j=1,..,r$ as $\alpha = A\,\theta$ where A is a (p×m) auxiliary matrix of constants and θ is an (m×r) matrix of coefficients. Let the matrix B be the orthogonal complement of A, that is, $B'A=0$. Then the weak exogeneity hypothesis can be written as $B'\alpha = 0$. As an example suppose we want to test for the possible weak exogeneity of the exchange rate in any of the three VAR systems. In terms of the elements of the loadings matrix α, this hypothesis can be written as, $\alpha_{1,j} = 0$, $j = 1,\dots,r$. In this case, the A and B matrices would be,

$$A = \begin{bmatrix} 0&0&0&0&0&0&0&0 \\ 1&0&0&0&0&0&0&0 \\ 0&1&0&0&0&0&0&0 \\ 0&0&1&0&0&0&0&0 \\ 0&0&0&1&0&0&0&0 \\ 0&0&0&0&1&0&0&0 \\ 0&0&0&0&0&1&0&0 \\ 0&0&0&0&0&0&1&0 \\ 0&0&0&0&0&0&0&1 \end{bmatrix} \quad B = \begin{bmatrix} 1 \\ 0 \\ 0 \\ 0 \\ 0 \\ 0 \\ 0 \\ 0 \\ 0 \end{bmatrix}.$$

Premultiplying (4.IV.1) by A' and B' respectively and substituting $\Pi=\alpha\beta'$ and $B'\alpha = 0$ or $\alpha = A\theta$ one gets,

$$A'H_{0t} = A'A\theta\beta'H_{1t} + A'\Gamma H_{kt} + A'\varepsilon_t \tag{II.3}$$

$$B'H_{0t} = B'\Gamma H_{kt} + B'\varepsilon_t, \tag{II.4}$$

where the second set of equations describes the dynamics of the weakly exogenous variables and the first set of equations the dynamics of the other variables. From (II.4) one can easily see why $B'H_{0t} = B'\Delta X_t$ is weakly exogenous for β, by simply noting that the pdf of H_{0t} conditional on $\mathbb{Z}_t = (H'_{1t}, H'_{kt})'$ is,

$$\begin{bmatrix} B'H_{0t} \\ A'H_{0t} \end{bmatrix} \sim N \left[\begin{pmatrix} B'\Gamma H_{kt} \\ A'A\theta\beta'H_{1t} + A'\Gamma H_{kt} \end{pmatrix} ; \begin{pmatrix} B'\Lambda B & B'\Lambda A \\ A'\Lambda B & A'\Lambda A \end{pmatrix} \right].$$

The density of $A'H_{0t}$ conditional on $B'H_{0t}$ and $\mathbb{Z}_t$ is given by,

$$N \left[(A'A\theta\beta'H_{1t} + A'\Gamma H_{kt} + \Lambda_{AB}\Lambda_{BB}^{-1}B'(H_{0t} - \Gamma H_{kt})); \tilde{\Lambda} \right]$$

where $\Lambda_{AB} = A'\Lambda B$ and $\tilde{\Lambda} = \Lambda_{AA} - \Lambda_{AB}\Lambda_{BB}^{-1}\Lambda_{BA}$. On the other hand, the marginal density of $B'H_{0t}$ conditional on $\mathbb{Z}_t$ can be written as,

$$N\ [(B'\Gamma H_{kt});\ \Lambda_{BB}].$$

One can now decompose the joint density into the product of the density of $A'H_{0t}$ conditional on $B'H_{0t}$ and Z_t,

$$L(A'H_{0t} \mid B'H_{0t},\ Z_t;\ A'\Gamma,\ A'\alpha\beta,\ \Lambda_{AB}\Lambda_{BB}^{-1},\ \tilde{\Lambda})$$

times the marginal density of $B'H_{0t}$ conditional on Z_t,

$$L(B'H_{0t} \mid Z_t;\ B'\Gamma,\ \Lambda_{BB}).$$

From the theory of the multivariate normal distribution the parameters $\Lambda_{AB}\Lambda_{BB}^{-1}$, Λ_{BB} and $\tilde{\Lambda}$ are variation free, so that the decomposition of the joint density into the product of the conditional and the marginal operates a sequential cut in the parameter space. Following Engle et al. (1983) $B'H_{0t}$ is weakly exogenous for $A'\Gamma$ and $A'\alpha\beta$.

Therefore, equation (II.4) can be written for the choice of A and B described above as,

$$\Delta x_{1t} = \gamma_1'\Delta X_{t-1} + \ldots + \gamma_{k-1}'\Delta X_{t-k+1} + \mu_1 + \phi' D_t + \varepsilon_{1t}$$

where γ_1', γ_{k-1}', μ_1 and ϕ' are the first rows of Γ_1, Γ_{k-1}, μ and Φ respectively, and Δx_{1t}, ε_{1t} are the first elements of ΔX_t and ε_t respectively. It is now clearly seen that stationary deviations from the long run relationships do not affect the short run dynamics of the weakly exogenous variables through the error correction term.

III. Testing for Weak Exogeneity

The likelihood ratio test statistic of the hypothesis $H_0: \alpha_{ij}=0$ for $j=1,\ldots,r$ against the alternative $H_1: \Pi=\alpha\beta'$ is given by

$T\sum_{i=1}^{r} \ln\{(1-\hat{\lambda}_{0i})/(1-\hat{\lambda}_{1i})\}$, where the λ_{1i}'s are the eigenvalues of the model under H_1 and the λ_{0i}'s are the roots of characteristic equation,

$$|\lambda S_{11.b} - S_{1a.b}S_{aa.b}^{-1}S_{a1.b}| = 0.$$

Where the $S_{ij.b}$ matrices are defined by, $S_{ij.b} = T^{-1}\sum_{t=1}^{T} \tilde{R}_{it}\tilde{R}'_{jt}$, $(i,j=a,1)$, $\tilde{R}_{at} = A'(I-S_{00}B(B'S_{00}B)^{-1}B')R_{0t}$ and $\tilde{R}_{1t} = R_{1t} - S_{10}B(B'S_{00}B)^{-1}B'R_{0t}$. The likelihood ratio statistic has an asymptotic distribution that was shown by Johansen (1991a) to be a χ^2 with $r(p-m)$ degrees of freedom.

Table I of appendix A summarizes the test for weak exogeneity of all the variables in the three systems. In all three systems we cannot reject the hypothesis that the exchange rate is weakly exogenous with respect to the cointegrating vectors. In addition, the US output in the Germany / US system and the British output in the UK / US system are also weakly exogenous with respect to the cointegrating vectors.

Thus, the short run dynamics of the exchange rate are not affected by transitory deviations from the long run equilibrium relationships.

IV. The Asset Market View Derived from an Error Correction Model

In this section we show how one can derive the *asset market view* of exchange rate determination derived from an ECM.

Let us consider the first equation of the ECM (II.1),

$$\Delta s_t = \pi_1' X_{t-1} + \gamma_{11}'\Delta X_{t-1} + \ldots + \gamma_{1k-1}'\Delta X_{t-k+1} + \mu_1 + \phi_1' D_t + \varepsilon_{1t}, \qquad \text{(IV.1)}$$

where Δs_t, μ_1 and ε_{1t} are the first components of ΔX_t, μ and ε_t and π_1', $\gamma_{11}', \ldots, \gamma_{1k-1}'$ and ϕ_1' the first rows of Π, $\Gamma_1, \ldots, \Gamma_{k-1}$ and Φ

respectively.

We have found the coefficients $\gamma_{11}',\ldots,\gamma_{1k-1}'$ and ϕ_1' to be not significantly different from zero. If this is the case, the short run dynamics of the exchange rate simplify and we can rewrite the first equation of the ECM as,

$$\Delta s_t = \pi_1' X_{t-1} + \mu_1 + \varepsilon_{1t}. \qquad \text{(IV.2)}$$

Writing the first row of Π as $\pi_1' = (\pi_{11}, \pi_{12}')$ and $X_t = (s_t,\ X_{2t}')'$ we can rewrite equation (V.2) as,

$$\Delta s_t = \pi_{11} s_{t-1} + \pi_{12}' X_{2t-1} + \mu_1 + \varepsilon_{1t}. \qquad \text{(IV.3)}$$

Leading equation (IV.3) one period ahead, taking mathematical expectations conditional on time t information set and rearranging, we get,

$$s_t = F_t + (1/\pi_{11})\ E_t(\Delta s_{t+1}). \qquad \text{(IV.4)}$$

Where the term $F_t = (\pi_{12}' X_{2t} + \mu_1)/\pi_{11}$ can be interpreted as the fundamentals. Formally, we have to require $\pi_{11} \neq 0$. This, in turn, implies that $\pi_{11} = \sum_{j=1}^{r} \alpha_{1j} \beta_{1j} \neq 0$. Note that weak exogeneity of the the exchange rate is sufficient for $\pi_{11} = 0$.

In the light of the evidence presented on the previous section where we found that the exchange rate is weakly exogenous, we have to admit that the ECM that we have fitted to the data is not compatible with the asset market model. However, one can always argue that the asset market model does not obtain because our choice of information set (data set) is not adequate.

The difference between our specification and those of Finn (1986), Woo (1985), Diebold (1986) and Wolff (1988) is that we allow $X_t' =$

$(s_t, X'_{2,t})$ to follow a cointegrated VAR whereas they assumed less general processes for the fundamentals. In particular, Finn (1986) allows for univariate ARIMA models for the fundamentals, Diebold (1986) lets some combinations of the fundamentals to follow a stationary VAR, Wolff postulates a stationary VAR model for the fundamentals in the relative form of equation (2.II.5). Finally, Woo (1985) postulates a stationary VAR for the exchange rate and some combinations of the fundamentals.

V. Conclusions

In this chapter we have analyzed the short run dynamics of the exchange rate. We saw how the error correction term does not enter the equations of the weakly exogenous variables in the ECM. The empirical evidence suggests that the exchange rates analyzed are weakly exogenous with respect to the cointegrating vectors. Thus they do not react to deviations from the long run relationships. In the last section we derive the asset market view from an ECM. Weak exogeneity of the exchange rates implies that the asset market model does not obtain.

APPENDIX A

Table I. Tests for Weak Exogeneity.

	Germany / US.	Japan / US.	UK / US.
s	1.612	8.000	7.315
m_*	15.407[a]	43.003[a]	22.548[a]
m	12.903[a]	24.705[a]	12.749[b]
y_*	9.937[b]	13.921[c]	5.579
y	1.641	12.886[c]	18.055[a]
i_*	20.840[a]	19.190[a]	11.532[b]
i	9.210[c]	24.437[a]	17.105[a]
π_*	28.879[a]	35.575[a]	22.469[a]
π	15.266[a]	29.988[a]	16.511[a]

a = significant at the 1 % level

b = significant at the 2.5 % level

c = significant at the 5 % level

d = significant at the 10 % level.

Chapter 6. Effect of Non-Normal Disturbances on Likelihood Ratio Tests

I. Introduction

Since Granger (1981) first introduced the concept of cointegration the field has experienced a great development. There are by now several methods of estimating cointegrating vectors: Ordinary Least Squares (Engle and Granger (1987)), Non-linear Least Squares (Stock (1987)), Principal Components (Stock and Watson (1988)), Canonical Correlations (Bossaerts (1988)) and full information maximum likelihood in a Gaussian system (Johansen (1988b, 1991a)). All these methods of estimation are fairly simple to implement and this is probably why empirical applications grow in number very quickly. Inference, on the other hand, is more difficult to carry out. All known hypotheses tests on the number of cointegrating vectors have non standard asymptotic distributions. In addition, only the ML procedure[1] allows the user to carry out inference on the cointegrating vectors and loading matrix based on standard χ^2 tests.

The small sample performance of the five methods named above has been studied by Gonzalo (1989). He finds that the ML estimator outperforms[2] the others, and furthermore, it is robust[3] to non-normal

---

1 Johansen (1991a) has derived likelihood ratio and Wald tests of hypotheses about the cointegrating vectors and the loadings matrix.

2 In terms of mean squared error and bias.

3 In the sense that its small sample performance is not

disturbances, ARCH effects and overparameterization of the lag structure. As Gonzalo points out, the robustness of this estimator to non-normality is not surprising since it can also be derived as a reduced rank regression estimator, for which the assumption of normality is not needed.

Johansen's procedure of estimating cointegrating vectors has therefore the double attraction of excellent small sample performance and robustness to departures from normality and homoskedasticity. However, all the hypotheses tests developed by Johansen are likelihood ratio tests and thus strongly rely on the assumed probability distribution of the disturbance term. This chapter studies the effect of non-normal disturbances and ARCH effects on those likelihood based tests.

We carry out a simulation exercise where the disturbance term is generated from several non-normal distributions (Uniform, Students's t, Cauchy and a Mixture of a normal and a χ^2 distribution) as well as from a heteroskedastic conditional distribution and compare the empirical finite sample distribution of the tests statistics with their theoretical asymptotic distribution under the assumption of normality. First the distribution of these test statistics are generated under the null and the empirical and theoretical size of the tests are compared. Secondly, the distributions of those test statistics are generated under local alternatives and the probability of type II error computed.

In section II we describe the Data Generating Process (DGP) that is used in the simulation. Section III analyzes the hypotheses and

---

affected by deviations from normality.

test statistics. Section IV summarizes how the simulations were carried out and reports the outcomes of those simulations. Finally, section V concludes.

II. The Data Generating Process

The data generating process used for the simulation is a slight modification of the one used by Banerjee, et al. (1986), Engle and Granger (1987) and Gonzalo (1989). It is as follows,

$$\begin{aligned} y_t - b\,x_t = z_t \quad &; \quad z_t = \rho\, z_{t-1} + e_{z_t} \\ a\,y_t - c\,x_t = w_t \quad &; \quad w_t = \gamma\, w_{t-1} + e_{w_t} \end{aligned} \tag{II.1}$$

where e_{z_t} and e_{w_t} are white noise disturbances.

From the DGP we may derive the structural form of the Error Correction Model (ECM) as,

$$\begin{bmatrix} 1 & -b \\ a & -c \end{bmatrix} \begin{bmatrix} \Delta y_t \\ \Delta x_t \end{bmatrix} = \begin{bmatrix} (\rho-1) & 0 \\ 0 & (\gamma-1) \end{bmatrix} \begin{bmatrix} z_{t-1} \\ w_{t-1} \end{bmatrix} + \begin{bmatrix} e_{z_t} \\ e_{w_t} \end{bmatrix}. \tag{II.3}$$

Let us denote the matrix in the left hand side of (II.3) by B_0, and assume $|B_0| \neq 0$. Then we can derive the reduced form ECM by simply premultiplying (II.3) by B_0^{-1},

$$\begin{bmatrix} \Delta y_t \\ \Delta x_t \end{bmatrix} = \begin{bmatrix} \alpha_{11} & \alpha_{12} \\ \alpha_{21} & \alpha_{22} \end{bmatrix} \begin{bmatrix} 1 & -b \\ a & -c \end{bmatrix} \begin{bmatrix} y_{t-1} \\ x_{t-1} \end{bmatrix} + \begin{bmatrix} u_{1t} \\ u_{2t} \end{bmatrix}, \tag{II.4}$$

where the elements of the weighting matrix α are,

$$\alpha_{11} = c\ (1-\rho)\ /\ (ab - c),\ \alpha_{21} = a\ (1-\rho)\ /\ (ab - c),$$

$$\alpha_{12} = b\ (\gamma - 1)\ /\ (ab - c),\ \alpha_{22} = (\gamma - 1)\ /\ (ab - c),$$

and the reduced form disturbances are,

$$\begin{bmatrix} u_{1t} \\ u_{2t} \end{bmatrix} = B_0^{-1} \begin{bmatrix} e_{z_t} \\ e_{w_t} \end{bmatrix}.$$

Finally, we derive the reduced form VAR representation of this DGP as,

$$\begin{bmatrix} y_t \\ x_t \end{bmatrix} = \begin{bmatrix} 1+\alpha_{11} + a\alpha_{12} & -(b\alpha_{11} + c\alpha_{12}) \\ \alpha_{21} + a\alpha_{22} & 1-(b\alpha_{21} + c\alpha_{22}) \end{bmatrix} \begin{bmatrix} y_{t-1} \\ x_{t-1} \end{bmatrix} + \begin{bmatrix} u_{1t} \\ u_{2t} \end{bmatrix}, \qquad \text{(II.5)}$$

which will be the actual form of the DGP used in the simulation.

Using a more compact notation we can write (II.5) as,

$$X_t = \Pi_1 X_{t-1} + U_t, \qquad \text{(II.6)}$$

where $X_t = (y_t, x_t)'$ and $U_t = (u_{1t}, u_{2t})'$. Let us now define the matrix polynomial $\Pi(L) = I - \Pi_1 L$ and the long run impact matrix,

$$\Pi = -\Pi(1) = -I + \Pi_1. \qquad \text{(II.7)}$$

Gonzalo (1989) uses this DGP in his Monte Carlo study to examine the finite sample properties of Johansen's estimator of cointegrating vectors when the errors are non-Gaussian. We will use that DGP to study the finite sample performance of the likelihood ratio tests for a series of hypotheses about cointegrating vectors and their loadings in a VAR when the gaussianity hypothesis is relaxed. In addition, the effect of ARCH disturbances upon these tests is also analyzed. Both deviations from the ideal iid Gaussian case are related since it is known that the unconditional distribution of the disturbances becomes non-normal in the presence of ARCH effects.

III. Hypotheses Tests

In this section we summarize the ML estimation and testing procedure developed by Johansen (1988b) for the particular case of the DGP that we have described in the previous section.

III.1. Tests on the Number of Cointegrating Vectors

The completely unrestricted model (II.5) can be written as,

$$H_1:\ \Delta X_t = \Pi\, X_{t-1} + U_t,\quad \Pi \text{ unrestricted.} \qquad \text{(III.1)}$$

Under this hypothesis $|\rho| < 1$ and $|\gamma| < 1$, so that rank(Π) = 2. Therefore, both variables are stationary in levels and there are no unit roots in the system.

Let us consider now the null hypothesis that there is one unit root, $\gamma = 1$, or equivalently, one cointegrating vector, $\beta = (1, -b)$. In this case Π is of reduced rank, rank(Π) = 1 and we can express this as,

$$H_2:\ \Pi = \alpha\, \beta'. \qquad \text{(III.2)}$$

where α is now a (2×1) matrix of unit rank, $\alpha' = (\alpha_1, \alpha_2)$. Under this hypothesis the variables, x_t and y_t, are difference stationary, I(1), but a linear combination $y_t - b\, x_t = z_t$ is stationary in levels, I(0), provided $|\rho| < 1$. The corresponding ECM under H_2 is,

$$\begin{bmatrix} \Delta y_t \\ \Delta x_t \end{bmatrix} = \begin{bmatrix} \alpha_1 \\ \alpha_2 \end{bmatrix} \begin{bmatrix} 1 & -b \end{bmatrix} \begin{bmatrix} y_{t-1} \\ x_{t-1} \end{bmatrix} + \begin{bmatrix} u_{1t} \\ u_{2t} \end{bmatrix} \tag{III.3}$$

or in a more compact notation,

$$\Delta X_t = \alpha\beta' X_{t-1} + U_t . \tag{III.4}$$

In order to derive the likelihood ratio test for the hypothesis H_2 against H_1 we assume U_t to be an i.i.d. series drawn from a N (0, Λ).

The model (III.4) can be written as,

$$H_{0t} = \alpha\ \beta' H_{1t} + U_t , \tag{III.5}$$

where $H_{0t} = \Delta X_t$ and $H_{1t} = X_{t-1}$.

The likelihood function of the model (III.5) is,

$$|\Lambda|^{-T/2}\exp\left\{-(1/2)\sum_{t=1}^{T}(H_{0t} - \alpha\beta' H_{1t})'\Lambda^{-1}(H_{0t} - \alpha\beta' H_{1t})\right\}.$$

For given β, the ML estimator of α is found by regression as,

$$\alpha = S_{01}\beta(\beta' S_{11}\beta)^{-1}.$$

For given β, Λ is found as,

$$\Lambda = S_{00} - S_{01}\beta(\beta' S_{11}\beta)^{-1}\beta S_{10},$$

where we have defined the cross products matrices,

$$S_{ij} = T^{-1}\sum_{t=1}^{T} H_{it} H'_{jt}, \quad \text{for } i,j = 0,1.$$

Finally, after substitution of Λ in the likelihood function, this becomes proportional to,

$$|\Lambda|^{-T/2} = |S_{00} - S_{01}\beta(\beta' S_{11}\beta)^{-1}\beta S_{10}|^{-T/2}$$

Thus, maximization of the likelihood function is equivalent to minimization of $|\Lambda|$ with respect to β. It can be shown that minimization of this determinant with respect to β can be performed by finding the r eigenvectors associated with the r largest eigenvalues that solve the characteristic equation,

$$|\lambda S_{11} - S_{10}S_{00}^{-1}S_{01}| = 0. \qquad \text{(III.6)}$$

Let us denote $\hat{\lambda}_i$, i = 1, 2 the eigenvalues of (III.6), where $\hat{\lambda}_1 > \hat{\lambda}_2$. Then the maximized likelihood function under H_2 is,

$$L_2^{-2/T} = |S_{00}| \ (1 - \hat{\lambda}_1).$$

Equivalently, the maximized likelihood function under H_1 is,

$$L_1^{-2/T} = |S_{00}| \ (1 - \hat{\lambda}_1) \ (1 - \hat{\lambda}_2).$$

Thus, the likelihood ratio tests of the hypothesis H_2: $\Pi = \alpha\beta'$, against the alternative H_1: Π unrestricted, is given by,

$$-2 \ln (L_1/L_2) = - T \ln (1-\hat{\lambda}_2). \qquad \text{(III.7)}$$

The asymptotic distribution of this likelihood ratio test statistic is not standard and given by (see Johansen (1988b)),

$$\left\{\int_0^1 (dB)B\right\}^2 / \left\{\int_0^1 B^2 \, dt\right\} \qquad \text{(III.8)}$$

where, B(t) is a one-dimensional Brownian motion. This is just the square of the usual asymptotic distribution of Dickey and Fuller's (1979) unit root test. The distribution of (III.8) has been tabulated by Johansen (1988b).

III.2. Tests of Linear Restrictions on the Cointegrating Vector

We can be interested in testing linear restrictions on β expressed as,

$$H_4 : \beta = J \varphi, \qquad \text{(III.9)}$$

where J is a known (2x1) vector and φ is an unknown scalar parameter. Because in this case there is just one cointegrating vector, under H_4 the cointegrating space is fully specified. In the simulation exercise we will use $J = (1, -1)'$, that is, the difference of the two variables is stationary. This will only be true when b = 1.

Estimation of the model under the hypothesis H_4: $\beta = J \varphi$, requires to solve the following eigenvalue problem,

$$|\lambda J'S_{11}J - J'S_{10}S_{00}^{-1}S_{01}J| = 0.$$

Let $\tilde{\lambda}$ be the only eigenvalue of this problem. Then, the likelihood ratio test of H_4 in H_2 is given by

$$-2 \ln (L_2/L_4) = T \ln \left\{(1-\tilde{\lambda})/(1-\hat{\lambda}_1)\right\}. \qquad \text{(III.10)}$$

The asymptotic distribution of this statistic is a χ^2 with one degree of freedom.

III.3. Tests of Restrictions on the Loadings Matrix

One may also be interested in testing hypotheses about the loadings matrix α of the form,

$$H_5:\ \alpha = A\ \psi, \tag{III.11}$$

where A is a known (2×1) vector and ψ is an unknown scalar parameter. In particular we will analyze the case A = (1, 0)', which implies that the error correction term does not enter the second equation of the ECM (III.3). This will only happen when a = 0, in which case the variable x is weakly exogenous with respect to β.

The particular case of hypothesis H_5: $\alpha = A\ \psi$, that we are interested in can be stated as H_5: $\alpha_2 = 0$ or $B'\alpha = 0$, where B = (0, 1) is the orthogonal complement of A.

The likelihood ratio test statistic of the hypothesis H_5 against the alternative H_2 is given by,

$$-2\ \ln\ (L_2/L_5) = T\ \ln \left\{(1-\bar{\lambda}_1)/(1-\hat{\lambda}_1)\right\} \tag{III.12}$$

where $\bar{\lambda}_1 > \bar{\lambda}_2 = 0$ are the eigenvalues that solve the characteristic equation,

$$|\lambda\ S_{11.b} - S_{1a.b} S_{aa.b}^{-1} S_{a1.b}| = 0. \tag{III.13}$$

The $S_{ij.b}$ matrices are defined by, $S_{ij.b} = T^{-1}\sum_{t=1}^{T} \tilde{H}_{it}\tilde{H}'_{jt}$, (i, j=a, 1) and $\tilde{H}_{at} = A'(I-S_{00}B(B'S_{00}B)^{-1}B')H_{0t}$ and $\tilde{H}_{1t} = H_{1t} - S_{10}B(B'S_{00}B)^{-1}B'H_{0t}$. The asymptotic distribution of (III.12) is given by a χ^2 with one degree of freedom.

IV. The Simulation Exercise

We generate random drawings from five different zero mean non-normal probability distributions for u_{1t} and u_{2t}. In all cases u_{1t}

and u_{2t} are generated independently.

(i) A Students's t probability distribution with three degrees of freedom. This distribution has thicker tails than the normal distribution and this is something that has been found in empirical work, specially in the case of the distribution of asset returns and exchange rates.

(ii) A Cauchy distribution. The departure from normality in this case is similar to the previous one, but it has fatter tails and the effect of outlayers is stronger.

(iii) A Uniform distribution on the interval (-0.5,0.5). This probabilistic model evenly spreads the probability mass over a small range.

(iv) A probability distribution that is a mixture of a normal and a χ^2 distribution ($v_t = 0.8\ N(0,1) + 0.2\ \chi^2_{(2)} - 0.4$), so that we can analyze the effect of nonsymmetric probability distributions.

(v) For comparison we also simulate the distribution of the test statistics under the assumption of normally distributed disturbances. This allows us to compare the small sample distribution of the statistics with their asymptotic ones.

In addition, we also generate disturbances that follow a simple ARCH model of the form[4],

$$u_{1t} = v_{1t}((1 - \delta) + \delta\ u^2_{1t-1})^{-1/2} \qquad \text{(IV.1)}$$

$$u_{2t} = v_{2t}((1 - \delta) + \delta\ u^2_{2t-1})^{-1/2} \qquad \text{(IV.2)}$$

where v_{1t} and v_{2t} are independent N(0,1) and u_{10} and u_{20} were randomly

---

4 We follow Gonzalo (1989).

drawn from two independent N(0,1). The parameter δ is allowed to take two possible values $\delta = \{0.2, 0.8\}$ which correspond to *weak* and *strong* ARCH effects respectively. Note that the design is such that the unconditional variance is always constant at the value of one. Though the conditional distribution of the disturbances is normal, the unconditional one is not. ARCH disturbances are characteristic of many economic time series and this is why we include them in our analysis.

The simulations are done as follows. We draw N (N being the number of replications) samples of 400 observations each for u_{1t} and u_{2t}. Then, the values of X_t are generated using the VAR form (II.5) of the DGP and treated as the data based on which the tests statistics (III.7), (III.10) and (III.12) are computed.

The analysis is twofold. On the one hand we study the empirical size of the tests under deviations from normality. On the other, we compute the power of those tests under local alternatives.

IV.1. Empirical Size of the Tests

In the simulation exercise we generate the empirical distribution of the likelihood ratio test statistics (III.7), (III.10) and (III.12) under the corresponding null hypotheses H_2, H_4 and H_5. For this purpose the parameter space is restricted to lie in the subspace where $\gamma = 1$, $\rho = \{0.6, 0.9\}$, b = 1, a = 0, so that all three hypotheses are true. As mentioned above, as ρ approaches unity, the closer is the system to a non-cointegrated one. We simulate the distribution of the statistics for two values of ρ in order to analyze the effect of this parameter on the tests. In addition, the parameter c is set equal to 0.5 for all the simulation exercise. The number of replications used to compute the size of the tests is N = 5,000.

First we consider the test statistic for the number of cointegrating vectors (III.7). When the disturbances are normal, the distribution of that statistic is given by (III.8) which is a non-standard distribution that involves a one-dimensional Brownian motion. This asymptotic distribution has been tabulated by Johansen (1988b) who approximated the one-dimensional Brownian motion by a random walk. Using the critical values reported by Johansen we have computed the empirical size of the test statistic for the number of cointegrating vectors (III.7) under all the different distributional setups described above.

Had the disturbances deviated from normality in any of the specific ways mentioned above, the actual significance levels at which we would have been testing hypothesis H_2 are reported in Tables I and II. When disturbances are Cauchy the nominal size of the test is always smaller than those given by the critical values tabulated by Johansen. The other types of departures from normality, including the ARCH effects, have less effect on the empirical sizes. It is specially interesting to note that the case of non-symmetrically distributed errors does not affect the tests. This goes in the opposite direction from Johansen's intuition, who suggests, in his 1990 paper, that the deviations from symmetry should have more perverse effects on his methodology. These results are maintained regardless whether ρ is closer to unity (0.9) or farther away (0.6).

Next we analyze the effect of non-normal disturbances on the small sample distribution of the statistic (III.10) for testing linear hypothesis on the cointegrating vector. Tables III and IV summarize the results in this case. Again Cauchy disturbances are the ones that have worse effects on the nominal size of the test. The other types of deviations from normality do not change the actual significance levels by much. However it is interesting to note that when $\rho = 0.9$, all empirical sizes (apart from those for Cauchy disturbances) are larger than the theoretical ones. The reason is that we are testing a linear restriction on the cointegrating vector, but as ρ approaches unity, the cointegrating relationship becomes non-stationary.

Finally, we analyze the effects of deviations from normality on the test statistic (III.12) for testing restrictions on the loadings matrix. In particular we test the null hypothesis of weak exogeneity of the variable x with respect to the cointegrating vector. This implies a zero restriction in that matrix. The empirical size of this test under all setups are tabulated in Tables V and VI. This type of tests are most adversely affected by the Cauchy and ARCH disturbances. In both cases the nominal size of the test is far off the theoretical one. In general, Cauchy disturbances bias the size of the test downwards and ARCH disturbances upwards. However, if the ARCH effects are *weak* the empirical sizes are not that far away from those assuming normality.

IV.2. Power of the Tests

In this section we study the power of the three tests under deviations from their corresponding null hypotheses and departures from normality. The power of the test when the null is false is just one minus the probability of committing type II error.

The null and local alternative hypotheses of all three tests can be stated as:

$$H_2:\ \gamma = 1, \qquad H_2^*:\ \gamma = 1 + \frac{\lambda}{T^{1/2}}, \tag{IV.3}$$

$$H_4:\ b = 1 \qquad H_4^*:\ b = 1 + \frac{\lambda}{T^{1/2}}, \tag{IV.4}$$

$$H_5:\ a = 0 \qquad H_5^*:\ a = 0 + \frac{\lambda}{T^{1/2}}. \tag{IV.5}$$

In the power calculations we have considered $\lambda = -1$, $T = 400$, $\rho = 0.6$ and the number of replications was $N = 2,000$.

Let us consider the test for the number of cointegrating vectors (III.7). Table VIII reports the rejection frequencies obtained using statistic (III.7) when the alternative is true. The power of this test is very low when the disturbance term presents ARCH effects. The other types of departure from normality do not affect the probability of making type II error.

Tests of linear restrictions on the cointegrating vector lead to rejection frequencies quite similar to the ones corresponding to a gaussian system which is quite high. The cases of ARCH and mixture disturbances present lower power but the difference is not considerable. Table VIII summarizes these results.

To end the discussion, we now focus on table IX. It shows that the power of tests for restrictions on the loadings matrix is practically unaffected by departures from normality.

V. Conclusions

In this chapter, we have studied the small sample performance of the likelihood ratio tests derived by Johansen (1988, 1990) under departures from normality. These are tests on the number of cointegrating vectors, linear restrictions on the cointegrating vectors and restrictions on the loadings matrix. We have generated the empirical distributions of those test statistics assuming that the disturbance term has five different non normal distributions. Some of these distributions are still symmetric but have thicker tails (Cauchy, Student's t) or are flat (Uniform), others are non symmetric (mixture of a Normal and a χ^2). Another type of non-normality analyzed is the one associated with ARCH disturbances.

The likelihood ratio test for cointegration presents a smaller empirical size than the corresponding theoretical one when the disturbances are Cauchy distributed. Otherwise, the test statistic is quite robust. However, the power of the test against local alternatives is dramatically reduced in the presence of ARCH disturbances.

The size of the test for linear restrictions on the cointegrating vectors is biased downwards by Cauchy disturbances. However, the power in all cases is fairly high and quite similar to the Gaussian case.

Finally, the size of the test for restrictions on the loading matrix is adversely affected by Cauchy and, specially, ARCH disturbances. The effect of the latter is to double the size of the gaussian case. Nevertheless, departures from normality do not change the power of this test which is quite high.

APPENDIX A: Size of the Tests

A.1. Tests for Cointegration

Table I. Empirical Distribution of the Test Statistic (III.7), Under Deviations from Normality.

$\gamma = 1$, $a = 0$, $b = 1$, $c = 0.5$, $\rho = 0.9$.

Critical Values = d	0.6	2.9	4.2	5.3
$(\int_0^1 (dB)B)^2 / (\int_0^1 B^2 dt)$	0.50	0.10	0.05	0.025
Cauchy	0.4658	0.0722	0.0330	0.0186
Mixture	0.4908	0.1124	0.0530	0.0256
N(0,1)	0.4862	0.1058	0.0496	0.0270
Student's t	0.4952	0.1014	0.0424	0.0228
Uniform	0.4840	0.1100	0.0524	0.0308
ARCH-1	0.4914	0.1046	0.0476	0.0274
ARCH-2	0.4874	0.1056	0.0458	0.0246

Any entry in this table corresponds to the probability that the statistic (III.7) is greater or equal to the value d, when the probability distribution of the disturbance term is any of those in the left hand side column.

Table II. Empirical Distribution of the Test Statistic (III.7).

Under Deviations from Normality.

$\gamma = 1$, $a = 0$, $b = 1$, $c = 0.5$, $\rho = 0.6$.

Critical Values = d	0.6	2.9	4.2	5.3
$(\int_0^1 (dB)B)^2/(\int_0^1 B^2 dt)$	0.50	0.10	0.05	0.025
Cauchy	0.4608	0.0730	0.0326	0.0182
Mixture	0.4884	0.1104	0.0496	0.0260
N(0,1)	0.4818	0.1016	0.0472	0.0246
Student's t	0.4896	0.0988	0.0412	0.0220
Uniform	0.4766	0.1074	0.0516	0.0272
ARCH-1	0.4874	0.1016	0.0444	0.0252
ARCH-2	0.4838	0.1024	0.0442	0.0252

Any entry in this table corresponds to the probability that the statistic (III.7) is greater or equal to the value d, when the probability distribution of the disturbance term is any of those in the left hand side column.

A.2. Test of Linear Restrictions on The Cointegrating Vector

Table III. Empirical Distribution of Test Statistic (III.10),

Under Deviations from Normality.

$\gamma = 1$, $a = 0$, $b = 1$, $c = 0.5$, $\rho = 0.9$.

d	0.455	1.32	2.71	3.84	5.02	6.63
$\chi^2_{(1)}$	0.50	0.25	0.10	0.05	0.025	0.01
Cauchy	0.6016	0.2986	0.0880	0.0358	0.0152	0.0046
Mixture	0.5050	0.2520	0.1072	0.0560	0.0278	0.0120
N(0,1)	0.5156	0.2620	0.1124	0.0564	0.0306	0.0124
Student's t	0.5272	0.2698	0.1150	0.0594	0.0312	0.0106
Uniform	0.5042	0.2680	0.1118	0.0606	0.0288	0.0118
ARCH-1	0.5146	0.2670	0.1092	0.0582	0.0290	0.0124
ARCH-2	0.5344	0.2820	0.1242	0.0594	0.0314	0.0128

Any entry in this table corresponds to the probability that the statistic (III.10) is greater or equal to the value d, when the probability distribution of the disturbance term is any of those in the left hand side column.

Table IV. Empirical Distribution of Test Statistic (III.10),

Under Deviations from Normality.

$\gamma = 1$, $a = 0$, $b = 1$, $c = 0.5$, $\rho = 0.6$.

d	0.455	1.32	2.71	3.84	5.02	6.63
$\chi^2_{(1)}$	0.50	0.25	0.10	0.05	0.025	0.01
Cauchy	0.5992	0.2862	0.0788	0.0304	0.0114	0.0036
Mixture	0.4946	0.2436	0.0980	0.0480	0.0234	0.0098
N(0,1)	0.5034	0.2526	0.1024	0.0502	0.0256	0.0092
Student's t	0.4878	0.2374	0.0942	0.0494	0.0220	0.0080
Uniform	0.4964	0.2532	0.1074	0.0516	0.0226	0.0088
ARCH-1	0.5028	0.2538	0.1040	0.0484	0.0242	0.0080
ARCH-1	0.5132	0.2598	0.1050	0.0468	0.0210	0.0080

Any entry in this table corresponds to the probability that the statistic (III.10) is greater or equal to the value d, when the probability distribution of the disturbance term is any of those in the left hand side column.

A.3. Test for Weak Exogeneity

Table V. Empirical Distribution of Test Statistic (III.10),

Under Deviations from Normality.

$\gamma = 1$, $a = 0$, $b = 1$, $c = 0.5$, $\rho = 0.9$.

d	0.455	1.32	2.71	3.84	5.02	6.63
$\chi^2_{(1)}$	0.50	0.25	0.10	0.05	0.025	0.01
Cauchy	0.2708	0.1238	0.0612	0.0374	0.0250	0.0162
Mixture	0.4974	0.2506	0.1002	0.0508	0.0260	0.0112
N(0,1)	0.5174	0.2630	0.1050	0.0578	0.0308	0.0096
Student's t	0.5002	0.2592	0.1036	0.0524	0.0260	0.0102
Uniform	0.5184	0.2582	0.1058	0.0540	0.0280	0.0106
ARCH-1	0.5250	0.2732	0.1170	0.0626	0.0330	0.0146
ARCH-2	0.6298	0.4084	0.2352	0.1606	0.1124	0.0760

Any entry in this table corresponds to the probability that the statistic (III.12) is greater or equal to the value d, when the probability distribution of the disturbance term is any of those in the left hand side column.

Table VI. Empirical Distribution of Test Statistic (III.10).

Under Deviations from Normality.

$\gamma = 1$, $a = 0$, $b = 1$, $c = 0.5$, $\rho = 0.6$.

d	0.455	1.32	2.71	3.84	5.02	6.63
$\chi^2_{(1)}$	0.50	0.25	0.10	0.05	0.025	0.01
Cauchy	0.1728	0.0842	0.0472	0.0344	0.0064	0.0178
Mixture	0.4984	0.2462	0.0918	0.0430	0.0146	0.0074
N(0,1)	0.5128	0.2492	0.1050	0.0530	0.0170	0.0100
Student's t	0.4774	0.2354	0.0942	0.0522	0.0136	0.0114
Uniform	0.5044	0.2512	0.1012	0.0532	0.0144	0.0118
ARCH-1	0.5402	0.2894	0.1268	0.0714	0.0390	0.0188
ARCH-2	0.6798	0.4836	0.3268	0.2530	0.2008	0.1496

Any entry in this table corresponds to the probability that the statistic (III.12) is greater or equal to the value d, when the probability distribution of the disturbance term is any of those in the left hand side column.

Appendix B: Power of the Tests

B.1. Tests for Cointegration

Table VII. Rejection Frequencies of statistic (III.7) under local alternatives.

$\gamma = 0.95$, $a = 0$, $b = 1$, $c = 0.5$, $\rho = 0.6$.

d	0.6	2.9	4.2	5.3
Johansen	0.50	0.10	0.05	0.025
Cauchy	0.9975	0.9930	0.9905	0.9820
Mixture	1.0000	0.9985	0.9910	0.9670
N(0,1)	1.0000	1.0000	0.9930	0.9680
Student's t	1.0000	0.9990	0.9945	0.9735
Uniform	1.0000	1.0000	0.9940	0.9690
ARCH-1	0.5440	0.1760	0.1045	0.0660
ARCH-2	0.6700	0.3390	0.2545	0.2055

Any entry in this table corresponds to the probability that the statistic (III.7) is greater or equal to the value d, when the hypothesis H_2 is false and the probability distribution of the disturbance term is any of those in the left hand side column.

B.2. Test for Linear Restrictions on The Cointegrating Vector

Table VIII. Rejection Frequencies of statistic (III.10)

under local alternatives.

$\gamma = 1$, $a = 0$, $b = 0.95$, $c = 0.5$, $\rho = 0.6$.

Critical Values	0.455	1.32	2.71	3.84	5.02	6.63
$\chi^2_{(1)}$	0.50	0.25	0.10	0.05	0.025	0.01
Cauchy	0.9650	0.9315	0.9040	0.8855	0.8670	0.8490
Mixture	0.9910	0.9850	0.9665	0.9560	0.9440	0.9170
N(0,1)	0.9975	0.9940	0.9895	0.9835	0.9775	0.9680
Student's t	0.9905	0.9790	0.9660	0.9475	0.9300	0.9110
Uniform	0.9970	0.9960	0.9915	0.9885	0.9825	0.9775
ARCH-1	0.9965	0.9945	0.9900	0.9865	0.9780	0.9705
ARCH-2	0.9975	0.9940	0.9865	0.9825	0.9775	0.9725

Any entry in this table corresponds to the probability that the statistic (III.10) is greater or equal to the value d, when the hypothesis H_4 is false and the probability distribution of the disturbance term is any of those in the left hand side column.

B.3. Test for Weak Exogeneity

Table IX. Rejection Frequencies of statistic (III.13)

under local alternatives.

$\gamma = 1$, $a = -0.05$, $b = 1$, $c = -0.5$, $\rho = 0.6$.

Critical Values	0.455	1.32	2.71	3.84	5.02	6.63
$\chi^2_{(1)}$	0.50	0.25	0.10	0.05	0.025	0.01
Cauchy	0.9990	0.9975	0.9950	0.9935	0.9910	0.9890
Mixture	1.0000	1.0000	1.0000	1.0000	1.0000	1.0000
N(0,1)	1.0000	1.0000	1.0000	1.0000	1.0000	1.0000
Student's t	1.0000	1.0000	1.0000	1.0000	1.0000	1.0000
Uniform	1.0000	1.0000	1.0000	1.0000	1.0000	1.0000
ARCH-1	1.0000	1.0000	1.0000	1.0000	1.0000	1.0000
ARCH-2	0.9980	0.9970	0.9955	0.9935	0.9895	0.9885

Any entry in this table corresponds to the probability that the statistic (III.12) is greater or equal to the value d, when the hypothesis H_5 is false and the probability distribution of the disturbance term is any of those in the left hand side column.

Chapter 7. Estimation of The Time Series Model

I. Introduction

In this chapter we describe several methods of estimation under different restrictions on the parameters of the model. Johansen's estimation procedure is just one of the methods analyzed, corresponding to the case when only the long run parameters α and β are restricted. In addition, we also study other types of restrictions, namely, zero restrictions on the short run parameters of the ECM.

The organization of the chapter is as follows. First of all, it is explained how we can interpret the ECM as derived from a dynamic simultaneous equation model. We also analyze the moving average representation of this model and its properties. This representation is then used in order to find the common trends representation of the model as in Stock and Watson (1988). Section III describes the estimators of the model under several types of restrictions on the short and long run parameters. Under no restrictions the OLS is the BLUE. When only the short run dynamics are restricted efficient estimation requires to use the SURE estimator. Estimation with the long run restrictions requires the use of an estimator of the cointegrating vectors. We explain Johansen's procedure, but other types of estimators could also be applied. Finally, we analyze the estimation of the model under both short and long run type of restrictions. Ahn and Reinsel (1990, 1991) have derived an estimation procedure that we describe in this section for the case of the type of short run and long run restrictions considered in this chapter. Their procedure is based on an algorithm quite demanding computationally, specially if the dimension of the system and the number of lags require the estimation of a large number of parameters. We propose an alternative, simpler, estimation and testing procedure for this case.

II. Two Different Interpretations of the Time Series Model

The first interpretation of the time series model links this with the classical simultaneous equations econometric models and is due to Chow (1990). The multivariate time series model analyzed in chapter 5 can be thought of as an unrestricted reduced form of some linear dynamic simultaneous equation model of the form,

$$B_0\Delta X_t = B_1X_{t-1} + B_2\Delta X_{t-1} + \ldots + B_k\Delta X_{t-k+1} + m + \Psi D_t + e_t. \qquad \text{(II.1)}$$

The matrix B_0 is assumed to be nonsingular, so premultiplying (II.1) by B_0^{-1} gives the reduced form (4.II.4). Chow (1990) has recently pointed out that both (4.II.4) and (II.1) have the same number of cointegrating vectors since $\text{rank}(B_1) = \text{rank}(B_0\Pi) = \text{rank}(\Pi)$. Writing $B_1 = B_0\alpha\beta' = \alpha^*\beta'$ we see that the same cointegrating vectors enter the structural and reduced forms with different weights. If our interest centers on the estimation of the cointegrating vectors and not in the matrix B_0 we only have to specify the reduced form. On the other hand, by postulating a reduced form we avoid the possibility of making the kind of misspecification errors that usually arise when one imposes identification restrictions in the structural form of the model.

The second interpretation links the time series model with the structural time series models of Nerlove et al (1979) and Harvey (1989). Using Johansen's (1991a) version of Granger's representation theorem, we can write the process (4.II.4) in the moving average form,

$$\Delta X_t = C(L)(\varepsilon_t + \mu + \Phi D_t), \qquad \text{(II.2)}$$

where $C(z) = \sum_{i=0}^{\infty} C_i z^i$, for some exponentially decreasing matrices C_j and $C(0) = I_p$. The matrix C(1) has reduced rank (p-r), which is the number of stochastic trends. Any $p \times r$ matrix β which spans the null space of C(1) so that $\beta' C(1)=0$ will produce an $r \times 1$ time series $Y_t = \beta' X_t$ which is stationary. Thus, the columns of β will contain the cointegrating vectors. Let us write the matrix polynomial C(L) as,

$$C(L) = C(1) + (1-L)\, C^*(L), \qquad \text{(II.3)}$$

where $C^*(L)$ has all its roots outside the unit circle and is defined as,

$$C^*(L) = \sum_{j=0}^{\infty} \left(- \sum_{i=j+1}^{\infty} C_i \right) L^j.$$

Premultiplying (II.5) by β' we get,

$$(1-L)\, Y_t = \beta' C(1)(\varepsilon_t + \mu + \Phi D_t) + (1-L)\beta' C^*(L)(\varepsilon_t + \Phi D_t).$$

In order for Y_t to be a stationary process, $\beta' C(1)$ has to be zero so that,

$$Y_t = \beta' C^*(L)(\varepsilon_t + \Phi D_t).$$

Strictly speaking, the process Y_t is not covariance stationary since its mean, $E(Y_t) = \beta' C^*(L)\Phi D_t$, depends on t, while its autocovariance function does not. However, this dependence is only within a year so $E(Y_t) = E(Y_{t+\tau})$, where τ is the seasonal frequency (τ=4 for quarterly data, τ=12 for monthly data and so on). We will call such a process stationary.

We can find the common trends representation following Stock and Watson (1988). Substituting backwards in (II.2) and rearranging,

$$X_t = X_0 + C(L)\sum_{s=1}^{t}\varepsilon_s + C(L)\Phi \sum_{i=0}^{t-1} L^i D_t + t\mu_0,$$

and making use of the decomposition (II.3),

$$X_t = X_0 + C(1)\sum_{s=1}^{t}\varepsilon_s + C^*(L)\,\varepsilon_t + \Phi^+(L)D_t^+ + t\mu_0, \tag{II.4}$$

where $\Phi^+(L) = C(L)\Phi$ and $D_t^+ = \sum_{i=0}^{t-1} L^i D_t$. Because $C(1)$ has reduced rank $d = (p-r)$, there exists a $(p\times r)$ matrix α of rank r such that $C(1)\alpha = 0$. If $\alpha_\perp$ is a $(p\times d)$ matrix of rank d such that $\alpha_\perp'\alpha = 0$ then the matrix $A \equiv C(1)\alpha_\perp$ is of rank d. Define the matrices $H = (\alpha, \alpha_\perp)$ and $S = (0_r, I_d)$ so that $C(1)H = AS$. We are now in a position to rewrite (II.4) as,

$$X_t = X_0 + C(1)H\left(H^{-1}\mu t + H^{-1}\sum_{s=1}^{t}\varepsilon_s\right) + \Phi^+(L)D_t^+ + C^*(L)\,\varepsilon_t$$

$$= X_0 + A\,\theta_t + \Phi^+(L)D_t^+ + C^*(L)\varepsilon_t, \tag{II.5}$$

where $\theta_t = SH^{-1}\mu t + SH^{-1}v_t$, $v_t = \sum_{s=1}^{t}\varepsilon_s$ and θ_t follows a d-dimensional random walk with drift. To see this rewrite θ_{t-1} as $\theta_{t-1} = SH^{-1}\mu(t-1) + SH^{-1}v_{t-1}$ or $\theta_{t-1} + SH^{-1}\mu + SH^{-1}\varepsilon_t = SH^{-1}\mu t + SH^{-1}v_t$. Therefore,

$$\theta_t = \psi + \theta_{t-1} + \xi_t, \tag{II.6}$$

where $\psi = SH^{-1}\mu$ is $(d \times 1)$ vector of constant terms and $\xi_t = SH^{-1}\varepsilon_t$ is a d-variate white noise vector. The vector θ_t can be interpreted as a vector of common stochastic trends since there are less trends than variables in the system. Equations (II.5) and (II.6) define the common trends representation of X_t that expresses it as the sum of the common trends, transitory and seasonal components plus the initial conditions.

This interpretation of the time series X_t is referred to as *structural time series model* by Harvey (1989) or as *unobserved components models* by Nerlove et al. (1979).

III. Estimation of the Model

As it stands, the Error Correction Model (ECM) specified in (4.II.4) is highly overparameterized. We will reduce the number of parameters by restricting the model in a number of ways. Below, we analyze the estimation of (4.II.4) under four different kind of restrictions:

$\mathcal{H}_0$: Unrestricted model.

$\mathcal{H}_1$: Restricted short run dynamics: zero restrictions on $\Gamma_1,\dots,\Gamma_{k-1}$.

$\mathcal{H}_2$: Restricted long run dynamics: $\Pi = \alpha\beta'$.

$\mathcal{H}_3$: Restricted short and long run dynamics.

III.1. Unrestricted Model

The ECM (4.II.4) without any restriction imposed is just another way of writing the VAR model (4.II.1) with a different parameterization. The maximum likelihood estimator of that model is well known to be identical to the multivariate OLS estimator. The asymptotic distribution of the estimated parameters associated with first differences of X_t and the dummies is normal with the usual covariance matrix, whereas the distribution of the estimated μ and Π will be nonstandard and depend on integrals of multivariate brownian motions[1].

Ahn and Reinsel call this estimator the full rank estimator because the unrestricted OLS estimator of Π will generally be of full rank. In this case we are not incorporating the unit roots of the system, and therefore misspecifying the model. However, the OLS estimator is consistent.

III.2. Restricted Short Run Dynamics

The simplest case corresponds to model (4.II.1) where we allow for different lag lengths k_i in each equation $i = 1,\dots,p$, $(p=9)$. That model would be nested in $\mathcal{H}_0$ with $k = \max\{k_1, k_2,\dots, k_p\}$. The Ljung-Box[2] Q statistic can be used for testing against autocorrelation in the residuals from each equation.

Once the lag length for each equation has been chosen, one can further restrict the model by excluding those regressors in first differences whose t-statistics are not significantly different from zero. That is, run the regressions,

$$\Delta x_{it} = \pi_i' X_{t-1} + \gamma_{i1}'\Delta X_{t-1} + \dots + \gamma_{ik_i-1}'\Delta X_{t-k_i+1} + \mu_i + \phi_i' D_t + \varepsilon_{it}, \qquad \text{(III.1)}$$

where π_i' and ϕ_i' are the i-th rows of Π and Φ respectively and x_{it}, ε_{it} and μ_i are the i-th components of X_t, ε_t and μ respectively. Significance of the coefficients $\gamma_{i1},\dots, \gamma_{ik_i-1}$ can be tested using

---

1 See Sims, Stock and Watson (1990) and Ahn and Reinsel (1990).

2 $Q(1) = T(T+2)\sum_{\tau=1}^{1}(T-\tau)^{-1}r_\tau^2 \xrightarrow{d} \chi_1^2$, where r_τ^2 is the τ-lag autocorrelation.

standard asymptotic theory.

By imposing exclusion restrictions on the Γ's we can write the i-th equation of the ECM as,

$$\Delta x_{it} = \pi_i' X_{t-1} + \gamma_{i1}^{*\prime} Z_{t-1}^{i} + \ldots + \gamma_{ik_i-1}^{*\prime} Z_{t-k_i+1}^{i} + \mu_i + \phi_i' D_t + \varepsilon_{it}, \qquad \text{(III.2)}$$

where $Z_{t-j}^{i} = R_{ij} \Delta X_{t-j}$, R_{ij} being a matrix of zeros and ones such that Z_{t-j}^{i} contains only some of the p elements of ΔX_{t-j}. Equation (III.2) can be written in a more compact form,

$$\Delta x_{it} = X_{t-1}' \pi_i + Z_t^{i} \Gamma_i^{*} + \varepsilon_{it},$$

where, $Z_t^{i} = [Z_{t-1}^{i\prime}, \ldots, Z_{t-k_i+1}^{i\prime}, 1, D_t']$, $\Gamma_i^{*} = [\gamma_{i1}^{*\prime}, \ldots, \gamma_{ik_i-1}^{*\prime}, \mu_i, \phi_i']'$.

Stacking over equations we can write (III.2) as,

$$\Delta X_t = \mathbb{X}_{t-1} \mathrm{vec}(\Pi') + \mathbb{Z}_t \Gamma^{*} + \varepsilon_t \qquad \text{(III.3)}$$

where, $\mathbb{X}_{t-1} = (I_p \otimes X_{t-1}')$,

$$\mathbb{Z}_t = \begin{bmatrix} Z_t^1 & 0 & . & 0 \\ . & & . & 0 \\ . & & . & . \\ 0 & . & . & Z_t^p \end{bmatrix} \qquad \mathrm{vec}(\Pi') = \begin{bmatrix} \pi_1 \\ \vdots \\ \pi_p \end{bmatrix} \qquad \Gamma^{*} = \begin{bmatrix} \Gamma_1^{*} \\ \vdots \\ \Gamma_p^{*} \end{bmatrix}$$

If the regressors Z_{it} are the same for all the equations, as it is usually the case in an unrestricted VAR, (III.3) boils down to (4.II.4). Efficient estimation of the parameters of (III.3) follows the standard SURE technique. Thus, the SURE estimator is,

$$\begin{bmatrix} \mathrm{vec}(\Pi') \\ \Gamma^{*} \end{bmatrix} = \left\{ \sum_{t=1}^{T} \begin{bmatrix} \mathbb{X}_{t-1}' \\ \mathbb{Z}_t' \end{bmatrix} \Lambda^{-1} [\mathbb{X}_{t-1}, \mathbb{Z}_t] \right\}^{-1} \left\{ \sum_{t=1}^{T} \begin{bmatrix} \mathbb{X}_{t-1}' \\ \mathbb{Z}_t' \end{bmatrix} \Lambda^{-1} \Delta X_t \right\}$$

for known Λ. A feasible SURE estimator can be obtained by using a consistent estimate of Λ from the OLS residuals of the estimation of (4.II.4).

III.3. Restricted Long Run Dynamics

In this section we outline the methodology developed by Johansen (1988b, 1991a) to estimate the ECM (4.II.4) subject to the restrictions implied by the existence of cointegration, i.e., $\Pi=\alpha\beta'$.

In order to implement Johansen's procedure it is convenient to use the same notation of chapter 4. Rewrite (4.II.4) as,

$$H_{0t} = \alpha\beta' H_{1t} + \Gamma H_{kt} + \varepsilon_t \tag{III.4}$$

where $H_{0t} = \Delta X_t$, $H_{1t} = X_{t-1}$, $H_{kt} = [\Delta X'_{t-1}, \Delta X'_{t-2}, \ldots, \Delta X'_{t-k+1}, D'_t, 1]'$, and $\Gamma = [\Gamma_1, \Gamma_2, \ldots, \Gamma_{k-1}, \Phi, \mu]$.

The likelihood function $L(\alpha,\beta,\Gamma,\Lambda)$ for model (III.4) is proportional to,

$$|\Lambda|^{-T/2}\exp\left\{-(1/2)\sum_{t=1}^{T}(H_{0t} - \alpha\beta' H_{1t} - \Gamma H_{kt})'\Lambda^{-1}(H_{0t} - \alpha\beta' H_{1t} - \Gamma H_{kt})\right\}.$$

Maximization of the likelihood function with respect to Γ for given α, β and Λ, is equivalent to applying GLS to the system (III.4), which in turn is equal to applying OLS to each equation since the regressors are the same in all equations. Defining the following cross product matrices,

$$M_{ij} = T^{-1}\sum_{i=1}^{T} H_{it}H'_{jt}, \qquad i,j=0,1,k$$

the ML estimator of Γ for given α and β is $\Gamma = M_{0k}M_{kk}^{-1} - \alpha\beta' M_{1k}M_{kk}^{-1}$. Defining the residuals,

$$U_{0t} = H_{0t} - M_{0k}M_{kk}^{-1}H_{kt} \qquad U_{1t} = H_{1t} - M_{1k}M_{kk}^{-1}H_{kt},$$

the model (III.4) once we substitute for Γ may be rewritten as,

$$U_{0t} = \alpha\beta' U_{1t} + \varepsilon_t. \tag{III.5}$$

The residuals U_{0t} and U_{1t} are constructed from 2p auxiliary regressions. U_{0t} and U_{1t} are found from the regression of ΔX_t and X_{t-1} on $\Delta X_{t-1},\ldots,\Delta X_{t-k+1}$, D_t and a constant term.

The concentrated likelihood function $L(\alpha,\beta,\Gamma(\alpha,\beta),\Lambda) = L(\alpha,\beta,,\Lambda)$ is now proportional to,

$$|\Lambda|^{-T/2}\exp\left\{-(1/2)\sum_{t=1}^{T}(U_{0t} - \alpha\beta' U_{1t})'\Lambda^{-1}(U_{0t} - \alpha\beta' U_{1t})\right\}.$$

Also for given β, α is found by regression as,

$$\alpha = S_{01}\beta(\beta' S_{11}\beta)^{-1}.$$

For given β, Λ is found as,

$$\Lambda = S_{00} - S_{01}\beta(\beta' S_{11}\beta)^{-1}\beta S_{10},$$

where we have defined the cross products matrices, $S_{ij} = T^{-1}\sum_{t=1}^{T} U_{it}U_{jt}'$, for i, j = 0, 1. Finally, after substitution of Λ in the likelihood function renders this proportional to,

$$|\Lambda|^{-T/2} = |S_{00} - S_{01}\beta(\beta' S_{11}\beta)^{-1}\beta S_{10}|^{-T/2}$$

Thus, maximization of the likelihood function is equivalent to minimization of |Λ| with respect to β. It can be shown that minimization of this determinant with respect to β can be performed by finding the r eigenvectors associated with the r largest eigenvalues that solve the characteristic equation,

$$|\lambda S_{11} - S_{10} S_{00}^{-1} S_{01}| = 0. \tag{III.6}$$

Even though this estimator of the cointegrating vectors β has been found as a maximum likelihood estimator it can also be derived as the estimator of the reduced rank regression (III.5). In order to derive such an estimator the normality assumption is not needed[3].

Since the cointegrating vectors are not identified when r>1, an arbitrary normalization has to be chosen in order to have a unique parameterization. For estimation purposes the normalization chosen is irrelevant since the ML procedure is invariant to normalization. However, in order to find the asymptotic properties of the estimator it is necessary to impose one. Johansen (1991a) points out that a general type of normalization can be found by choosing a (pxr) matrix J such that $J'\beta$ has full rank defining the normalized estimator as, $\hat{\beta}_J = \hat{\beta}(J\hat{\beta})^{-1}$, where $\hat{\beta}$ is the ML estimator. Johansen chooses a normalization of the form, $J = (\beta'\beta)^{-1}\beta$ from which he finds an asymptotic representation for $\hat{\beta}_J$.

Johansen (1991a) has developed various likelihood ratio tests for linear restrictions on the cointegrating vectors β and the loadings matrix α and also for testing the number of cointegrating vectors. These test statistics are simple functions of the eigenvalues resulting from (III.6). Johansen has also shown that the asymptotic distribution of the properly normalized maximum likelihood estimator of β converges at a rate T to a mixture of integrals of multivariate brownian motion.

---

3 See Gonzalo (1989) and Velu, Reinsel and Wichern (1986).

Let us denote the ML estimators by $\tilde{\alpha}$, $\tilde{\beta}$ and $\tilde{\Gamma}$, then Lütkepohl and Reimers (1990) have shown that,

$$T^{1/2} \operatorname{vec} \{ [\tilde{\alpha}\tilde{\beta}, \tilde{\Gamma}] - [\alpha\beta, \Gamma] \} \xrightarrow{d} N(0, \Sigma)$$

where $\Sigma = (A'V^{-1}A) \otimes (S_{00} - \alpha\alpha')$ and,

$$A = \begin{pmatrix} I_{k(p-1)} & 0 \\ 0 & \beta' \end{pmatrix}, \quad V = \operatorname{plim} T^{-1} \sum_{t=1}^{T} \begin{pmatrix} \beta' X_{t-1} \\ H_{kt} \end{pmatrix} \begin{pmatrix} \beta' X_{t-1} \\ H_{kt} \end{pmatrix}'$$

A consistent estimate of Σ is given by $\tilde{\Sigma}$, where we have substituted α, β and Γ by their ML estimates, $\tilde{\alpha}$, $\tilde{\beta}$ and $\tilde{\Gamma}$.

Using the results of Stock (1987) one can show that the asymptotic distribution of the maximum likelihood estimator of the short run parameters α, $\Gamma_1,\ldots,\Gamma_{k-1}$, μ and Φ is identical to that of the multivariate OLS estimator applied to the system,

$$\Delta X_t = \alpha\, \hat{Y}_{t-1} + \Gamma_1 \Delta X_{t-1} + \ldots + \Gamma_{k-1} \Delta X_{t-k+1} + \mu + \Phi\, D_t + \varepsilon_t, \qquad \text{(III.7)}$$

where $\hat{Y}_{t-1} = \hat{\beta}' X_{t-1}$ and $\hat{\beta}$ is the maximum likelihood estimator of β. Note that this is still true when $\hat{\beta}$ is replaced by any consistent estimator of β. Furthermore, the covariance matrix of these estimator is consistently estimated by the usual OLS computer packages.

III.4. Restricted Short and Long Run Dynamics

III.4.1. Gaussian Reduced Rank Maximum Likelihood Estimator

In this section we consider the estimation of the ECM under restrictions in both short and long run dynamics. That is, we restrict some of the elements of $\Gamma_1,\ldots,\Gamma_{k-1}$ to be zero and, at the same time, constrain the long run impact matrix Π to be equal to $\alpha\beta'$.

Estimation of the ECM under restrictions on Π and $\Gamma_1,\ldots,\Gamma_{k-1}$ has been considered by Ahn and Reinsel (1988, 1990). However, they analyze *nested reduced rank* restrictions, i.e. rank $(\Gamma_1) = r_1 \geq \ldots \geq$ rank $(\Gamma_{k-1}) = r_{k-1}$, so that one can write $\Gamma_1 = A_1'B_1, \ldots, \Gamma_{k-1} = A_{k-1}'B_{k-1}$, where A_i and B_i are $(p\times r_i)$ matrices. We have not considered this type of nested reduced rank structure but just exclusion restrictions on the Γ_i's.

The ECM under $\mathcal{H}_4$ is,

$$\Delta X_t = \mathbb{X}_{t-1}\mathrm{vec}(\beta\alpha') + \mathbb{Z}_t\,\Gamma^* + \varepsilon_t. \tag{III.7}$$

Maximization of the log-likelihood for this model is equivalent to minimizing,

$$T\log|\Lambda| + \sum_{t=1}^{T}\varepsilon_t'\Lambda^{-1}\varepsilon_t.$$

Analytic solution to the minimization problem is not possible. However, Ahn and Reinsel (1990) propose a Gauss-Newton algorithm based on the iteration rule,

$$\theta^{(i+1)} = \theta^{(i)} - \left(\sum_{t=1}^{T} W_t'\Lambda^{-1}W_t\right)^{-1}\left(\sum_{t=1}^{T} W_t'\Lambda^{-1}\varepsilon_t\right), \tag{III.8}$$

where, in our case, $W_t' = \partial\varepsilon_t'/\partial\theta$, $\theta' = (\mathrm{vec}(\alpha')', \mathrm{vec}(\beta)', \Gamma^{*\prime})$, and,

$$-\frac{\partial\varepsilon_t'}{\partial\theta} = \begin{bmatrix} (I_p\otimes\beta')\,\mathbb{X}_{t-1}' \\ (\alpha'\otimes I_p)\,\mathbb{X}_{t-1}' \\ \mathbb{Z}_t' \end{bmatrix}.$$

Initial consistent estimates of Λ and θ are necessary to start up the algorithm. They are readily available from the estimators described in section III.3. The scheme (III.8) should be embedded within a step-wise procedure where Λ is updated after each iteration.

Without imposing a normalization previous to the implementation of the algorithm, there can be convergence problems since there are multiple local maxima. Ahn and Reinsel choose a normalization $J = (I_r, 0_{(p-r)})$, such that $\beta' = (I_r, b)$.

The asymptotic properties of this type of estimator have been analyzed by Ahn and Reinsel (1988) for the stationary case and in Ahn and Reinsel (1990) for the ECM of the form (III.7).

The limiting distribution of the likelihood ratio test for the number of cointegrating vectors under restrictions on the Γ's and Π has been derived by Reinsel and Ahn (1991). This asymptotic distribution is identical to the one obtained by Johansen (1988b, 1991a) for the case when no restrictions on the Γ's are placed. In addition, the asymptotic distribution of the maximum likelihood estimator of β is also the same as the one derived by Ahn and Reinsel (1990) for the situation when no constraints are imposed on the Γ's.

III.4.2. Two Step Procedure

The estimation procedure just described in the previous section is quite demanding computationally speaking. Specially when we analyze a system of high dimension with several lags. In this section we develop an alternative, much simpler, procedure.

The procedure is a slight modification of Engle and Granger's (1987) two-step method. It is as follows:

(i) In the first step we estimate the cointegrating vectors β using Johansen's procedure, without imposing the restrictions on the Γ's. As we have commented above, the asymptotic distribution of this estimator is identical as if we had imposed those restrictions. Furthermore, Gonzalo (1989) has carried out a Monte Carlo experiment where he shows how Johansen's ML estimator of the cointegrating vectors is robust to overparameterization of the ECM.

(ii) The second step uses the multivariate OLS estimator of the ECM,

$$\Delta X_t = \alpha \hat{Y}_{t-1} + Z_t \Gamma^* + \varepsilon_t \tag{III.9}$$

where $\hat{Y}_{t-1} = \hat{\beta}' X_{t-1}$ and $\hat{\beta}$ is the ML estimator defined in section III.3 and Γ^* incorporates the zero restrictions on the lagged differences of X_t.

Stock (1987) has shown that the asymptotic distribution of the OLS estimator of (III.9) is the same as if we knew the true value of β. Furthermore, since (III.9) involves only stationary variables, standard asymptotic theory applies for the estimates of α and Γ^*.

The difference between this and Engle and Granger's procedure is that we use Johansen's estimator rather than the OLS estimator of the cointegrating regression. However, both estimators are consistent and converge to their population counterparts at a rate T.

Chapter 8. Prediction in Cointegrated Systems

I. Introduction

A wide range of macroeconomic magnitudes can be characterized "as non-stationary processes that have no tendency to return to a deterministic path". This was reported by Nelson and Plosser (1982), but there is still a controversy about whether the nonstationarity of those variables can be captured by a deterministic or stochastic trend.

The theory of cointegration has opened a new door into the estimation of and inference about economic models. If we consider those nonstationary variables in a vector time series and find a number of stationary linear combinations among them, they may be interpreted as existing *long run equilibrium relationships*.

Most of the effort made by econometricians in this regard has been directed towards estimation and testing. Surprisingly, there is very little work done in the area of prediction in cointegrated systems despite its relevance. Engle and Yoo (1987) and Reinsel and Ahn (1991) are the only references, to the best of our knowledge. There is no more demanding test of an economic model than one where it is used for prediction. Moreover, if the variables in the model are nonstationary, the prediction is even more challenging. This is one of the main reasons why we study how to predict with a cointegrated time series model.

In order to motivate the analysis, let us consider a nonstationary p-dimensional time series X_t, which is assumed to become stationary after first differencing. However, it is also assumed that there are fewer unit roots than elements in the vector time series.

Let us consider the problem of forecasting with such a process. Since the vector time series is not stationary in levels, the Theory of optimal prediction with multivariate time series, as described by Granger and Newbold (1977), is not directly applicable. On the other hand, if the system were fully non-stationary with as many unit roots as variables, one could apply the above Theory after first differencing all its components. However, the later approach is not recommended when dealing with a partially non-stationary time series. Even though the theory of optimal prediction is applicable to the first differences of the multivariate time series, the procedure would be inefficient since first differencing eliminates some information. The optimal strategy is to transform the system into a process that is stationary and does not eliminate the information about cointegration.

There are several estimation methods of those partially non-stationary systems that incorporate the information provided by the cointegrating relationships. Engle and Granger (1987) two steps procedure, Stock (1987) nonlinear least squares method, Stock and Watson (1988) principal components approach and Johansen (1988b, 1991a) maximum likelihood estimation procedure are the most commonly used ones. These methods yield more efficient estimates of the partially non-stationary time series and therefore should produce better predictions.

Section II studies the properties of true forecasts generated by a cointegrated system. In section III we derive the asymptotic covariance matrix of the prediction errors.

II. Properties of the True Forecasts from a Cointegrated System

Engle and Yoo (1987) examined the behavior of multi-step

forecasts generated by a cointegrated system as defined by Engle and Granger (1987). Using a similar approach, we discuss the properties of those forecasts.

The vector time series X_t has an error correction (4.II.4) and a moving average (4.V.1) representations that fully characterize the dynamics of the series and do incorporate all the information about cointegration. Either of these two representations specify a stationary process for ΔX_t to which the Theory of optimal prediction (Granger and Newbold (1977 ch.7) can be applied.

Let us rewrite (7.II.2) and, without loss of generality, drop the seasonal component so that $\Phi = 0$,

$$X_t = X_{t-1} + \sum_{i=0}^{\infty} C_i \varepsilon_{t-i} + \mu_0, \qquad \text{(II.1)}$$

where $\mu_0 = C(L)\mu = C(1)\mu$ so that $\beta'\mu_0 = 0$. Assuming $\varepsilon_i = 0 \;\; \forall\, i \le 0$ and X_0 is a fixed constant. Backwards substitution in (II.1) yields,

$$X_t = X_0 + \sum_{i=1}^{t} \sum_{j=0}^{t-i} C_j \varepsilon_i + t\mu_0,$$

so that for $h \ge 1$,

$$X_{t+h} = X_0 + \sum_{i=1}^{t+h} \sum_{j=0}^{t+h-i} C_j \varepsilon_i + (t+h)\mu_0,$$

$$= X_0 + \sum_{i=1}^{t+h} B_i^{t+h} \varepsilon_i + (t+h)\mu_0, \qquad \text{(II.2)}$$

where $B_i^{t+h} = \sum_{j=0}^{t+h-i} C_j$.

Based on the information set $I_t = \{ X_0, \varepsilon_1, \ldots, \varepsilon_t \}$, the optimal forecast of X_{t+h} will be of the form,

$$f_{t+h} = X_0 + \sum_{i=1}^{t} \theta_i^{t+h} \varepsilon_i + (t+h)\mu_0.$$

Let e_{t+h} denote the forecast error, then we can write,

$$e_{t+h} = X_{t+h} - f_{t+h} = \sum_{i=1}^{t} (B_i^{t+h} - \theta_i^{t+h})\, \varepsilon_i + \sum_{i=t+1}^{t+h} B_i^{t+h}\, \varepsilon_i .$$

The optimal linear forecast is chosen so as to minimize the covariance matrix of prediction errors, $\Omega(h) = E(e_{t+h} e'_{t+h})$, in the matrix sense[1]. This criterion leads to the choice of weights $\theta_i^{t+h} = B_i^{t+h} = \sum_{j=0}^{t+h-i} C_j$.

Therefore, we can write the optimal forecast as,

$$f_{t+h} = X_0 + \sum_{i=1}^{t} \sum_{j=0}^{t+h-i} C_j \varepsilon_i + (t+h)\mu_0 . \qquad \text{(II.3)}$$

The forecast error is,

$$e_{t+h} = \sum_{i=1}^{h} \sum_{j=0}^{t+h-i} C_j \varepsilon_i .$$

And the covariance matrix of forecast errors is,

$$\Omega(h) = \sum_{i=1}^{h} \left[\left(\sum_{j=0}^{t+h-i} C_j \right) \Lambda \left(\sum_{j=0}^{t+h-i} C'_j \right) \right] .$$

<u>Property 1:</u> Engle and Yoo (1987).

The vector of h-step-ahead forecasts f_{t+h} will satisfy the cointegration relations exactly in the long run.

In order to see this, let us premultiply (II.3) by the matrix of cointegrating vectors β,

---

1 See Granger and Newbold (1977).

$$\beta' f_{t+h} = \beta' X_0 + \beta' \sum_{i=1}^{t} \sum_{j=0}^{t+h-i} C_j \varepsilon_i . \qquad \text{(II.4)}$$

Where we have made use of $\beta' C(1)\mu = 0$. Taking limits when h tends to infinite and noting that $\lim_{h \to \infty} \sum_{j=0}^{t+h-i} C_j = C(1)$ we get,

$$\lim_{h \to \infty} \beta' f_{t+h} = \beta' X_0 + \beta' C(1) \sum_{i=0}^{t} \varepsilon_i = \beta' X_0 . \qquad \text{(II.5)}$$

For not very large h, $\sum_{j=0}^{t+h-i} C_j \cong C(1)$ since the matrices C_j form an exponentially decreasing sequence. Therefore, for a long enough horizon h, the *predicted equilibrium error* $\beta' f_{t+h}$ will be approximately equal to $\beta' X_0$. Therefore we can write,

$$\beta' f_{t+h} = \beta' X_0 + o(1), \qquad \text{(II.6)}$$

as h goes to infinity.

Property 2: The forecasts generated by a cointegrated VAR system follow a VAR in first differences for a long enough horizon.

The forecasts generated using the moving average representation (II.3) will also satisfy the ECM,

$$\Delta f_{t+h} = \alpha\beta' f_{t+h-1} + \Gamma_1 \Delta f_{t+h-1} + \ldots + \Gamma_{k-1} \Delta f_{t+h-k+1} + \mu, \qquad \text{(II.7)}$$

with $f_{t+h} = X_{t+h}$ for $h \le 0$. Substituting the approximation $\beta' f_{t+h-1} \cong \beta' X_0$ in (II.7) we obtain for some large enough h,

$$\Delta f_{t+h} \cong \Gamma_1 \Delta f_{t+h-1} + \ldots + \Gamma_{k-1} \Delta f_{t+h-k+1} + \mu^*, \qquad \text{(II.8)}$$

where $\mu^* = \mu + \alpha\beta' X_0$. In words, the forecasts generated by a cointegrated VAR system follow a VAR in first differences for a long enough horizon. This is a quite interesting result since the VAR in first differences is a misspecified model when there is cointegration. This, of course, does not mean that the VAR in first differences has to predict better than the restricted ECM.

III. Estimated Forecasts from a Cointegrated System

In this section we derive the asymptotic covariance matrix of the forecast errors. In order to do so we cast the model in state space form. Let us define the state vector,

$$Z_t = [\, X'_{t-1},\ \Delta X'_t,\ \Delta X'_{t-1}, \ldots,\ \Delta X'_{t-k+2},\ 1]'.$$

The measurement equation is,

$$X_t = [I_p,\ I_p,\ \mathbb{O}_p, \ldots,\ \mathbb{O}_p,\ 0_p]\ Z_t = S\ Z_t$$

where S is a $(p\times(p(k-1)+1))$ selection matrix, I_p is the $(p\times p)$ identity matrix, $\mathbb{O}_p$ is a $(p\times p)$ matrix of zeros and 0_p is a $(p\times 1)$ vector of zeros. The transition equation is,

$$Z_t = F\ Z_{t-1} + v_t, \qquad \text{(III.1)}$$

or more explicitly,

$$\begin{bmatrix} X_{t-1} \\ \Delta X_t \\ \Delta X_{t-1} \\ \vdots \\ \Delta X_{t-k+2} \\ 1 \end{bmatrix} = \begin{bmatrix} I_p & I_p & \mathbb{0}_p & \cdots & \mathbb{0}_p & 0_p \\ \Pi & (\Gamma_1 + \Pi) & \Gamma_2 & \cdots & \Gamma_{k-1} & \mu \\ \mathbb{0}_p & I_p & \mathbb{0}_p & \cdots & & 0_p \\ & & & & & \\ \mathbb{0}_p & \cdots & & I_p & \mathbb{0}_p & 0_p \\ 0'_p & \cdots & & & 0'_p & 1 \end{bmatrix} \begin{bmatrix} X_{t-2} \\ \Delta X_{t-1} \\ \Delta X_{t-2} \\ \vdots \\ \Delta X_{t-k+1} \\ 1 \end{bmatrix} + \begin{bmatrix} 0_p \\ \varepsilon_t \\ 0_p \\ \vdots \\ 0_p \\ 0 \end{bmatrix}$$

The actual value of X_t at period t+h can be written as,

$$X_{t+h} = S(F^h Z_t + \sum_{j=1}^{h} F^{h-j} v_{t+j}). \qquad \text{(III.2)}$$

The optimal forecast of X_{t+h} at time t is given by,

$$f_{t+h} = S\, F^h\, Z_t. \qquad \text{(III.3)}$$

In practice f_{t+h} has to be estimated by replacing the true values of the parameters by their sample counterparts. One can decompose the estimated prediction error as the sum of the estimation error and the true prediction error,

$$\tilde{e}_{t+h} = X_{t+h} - \tilde{f}_{t+h} = - (\tilde{f}_{t+h} - f_{t+h}) - (f_{t+h} - X_{t+h}),$$

where $\tilde{f}_{t+h}$ is the estimated forecast. Using the forecasting formulae (III.2) and (III.3) we can rewrite the expression above as,

$$\tilde{e}_{t+h} = - S\, (\tilde{F}^h - F^h)\, Z_t - S \sum_{j=1}^{h} F^{h-j}\, v_{t+j}$$

$$= \xi_{1h} + \xi_{2h}, \qquad \text{(III.4)}$$

where the two terms ξ_{1h} and ξ_{2h} are uncorrelated.

We are going to derive the asymptotic distribution of the estimated prediction error based on the asymptotic distribution of the maximum likelihood estimator of F. In order to do so, we require some preliminary results.

Let us stack the columns of the matrices defining ξ_{1h},

$$\mathrm{vec}(\xi_{1h}) = (Z_t' \otimes S)\ \mathrm{vec}\ (\tilde{F}^h - F^h). \tag{III.5}$$

Lemma 1 of Schmidt (1974) allows us to write,

$$(\tilde{F}^h - F^h) = \sum_{j=0}^{h-1} \tilde{F}^h(\tilde{F} - F)F^{h-1-j}$$

and therefore equation (III.5) becomes,

$$\mathrm{vec}(\xi_{1h}) = (Z_t' \otimes S) \sum_{j=0}^{h-1} (F'^{h-1-j} \otimes \tilde{F}^h)\ \mathrm{vec}\ (\tilde{F} - F). \tag{III.6}$$

Now we are in a position to derive the asymptotic distribution of vec $(\tilde{F} - F)$. Lütkepohl and Reimers (1990) have shown that Johansen's maximum likelihood estimator has the following asymptotic representation,

$$T^{1/2}\ \mathrm{vec}\ \{[\tilde{\alpha}\tilde{\beta},\ \tilde{\Gamma}] - [\alpha\beta,\ \Gamma]\} \xrightarrow{d} N\ (0,\ \Sigma), \tag{III.7}$$

where $\tilde{\Pi} = \tilde{\alpha}\tilde{\beta}$ and $\tilde{\Gamma}$ are the maximum likelihood estimators defined in section III.3 of chapter 7. Let us denote

$$(\tilde{P} - P) = \{[\tilde{\alpha}\tilde{\beta},\ \tilde{\Gamma}] - [\alpha\beta,\ \Gamma]\},$$

so that we can write,

$$(\tilde{F} - F) = D\ (\tilde{P} - P)\ E,$$

where the auxiliary matrices D and E are defined as,

$$D = \begin{bmatrix} \mathbb{O}_p \\ I_p \\ \mathbb{O}_p \\ \vdots \\ \mathbb{O}_p \\ 0'_p \end{bmatrix} \qquad E = \begin{bmatrix} I_p & I_p & \mathbb{O}_p & \cdots & \mathbb{O}_p & 0_p \\ \mathbb{O}_p & I_p & \mathbb{O}_p & \cdots & \mathbb{O}_p & 0_p \\ \mathbb{O}_p & \mathbb{O}_p & I_p & \cdots & \mathbb{O}_p & 0_p \\ \vdots & & & \ddots & \vdots & \vdots \\ \mathbb{O}_p & \cdots & & \cdots & I_p & 0_p \\ 0'_p & \cdots & & \cdots & 0'_p & 1 \end{bmatrix}$$

Therefore,

$$\text{vec}\,(\tilde{F} - F) = (E' \otimes D)\ \text{vec}\,(\tilde{P} - P).$$

And the desired asymptotic distribution is,

$$T^{1/2}\ \text{vec}(\xi_{1h}) \xrightarrow{d} N\,(0,\ M_1), \qquad \text{(III.8)}$$

$$M_1 = \text{plim}\ (Z'_t \otimes S)\ B_h\ (E' \otimes D)\ \Sigma\ (E \otimes D')\ B'_h\ (Z_t \otimes S'),$$

and $B_h = \sum_{j=0}^{h-1} (F'^{\,h-1-j} \otimes \tilde{F}^h)$.

On the other hand, the other term in (III.4) has a normal distribution with covariance matrix,

$$M_2 = E\ (\xi_{2h}\xi'_{2h}) = S \sum_{j=1}^{h} F^{h-j}\ V\ F'^{\,h-j}\ S', \qquad \text{(III.9)}$$

where V is the covariance matrix of the disturbance v_t of (III.1).

Finally, the asymptotic covariance matrix of the estimated prediction error is,

$$AE\ (\ddot{e}_{t+h}\tilde{e}'_{t+h}) = T^{-1}\ M_1 + M_2.$$

This matrix is the asymptotic mean squared error of an optimal predictor based on the asymptotically efficient estimator of the parameters of the model. Therefore it defines a lower bound of the asymptotic mean squared errors within the class of predictors based on consistent and asymptotically normal estimators.

Chapter 9. Nominal Exchange Rate Prediction

I. Introduction

Nominal exchange rate prediction interests many. Economists can use exchange rate prediction exercises as a way of validating structural models of exchange rate determination. Businessmen are interested in forecasting rates to the extent that this will allow them to better hedge against foreign exchange risk. Finally, governments will conduct their domestic economic policy guided by a better knowledge if they have accurate rate forecasts at their disposal.

In chapter 4 we found evidence about the existence of long run relationships (co-integrating vectors) that link exchange rates and their fundamentals. The long run relations impose some restrictions on the multivariate time series representation of the exchange rate and its fundamentals. In this chapter we continue using the same data set and study whether the imposition of those long run restrictions helps predicting those exchange rates. If the long run relationships have any bearing in short run exchange rate determination they should improve exchange rate forecasts at least with respect to the unrestricted multivariate time series model.

The organization of the chapter is as follows. Section II surveys the literature on the subject of exchange rate prediction. We use the multivariate time series model described in chapter 4 and estimate it under the restrictions on the short and long run dynamics described in chapter 7. In section III we present the results of the forecasting exercise. Section IV concludes.

II. Review of Literature

After the abandonment of the Bretton Woods system in 1973 exchange rate fluctuations attracted the attention of theorists who modeled them in diverse forms. Frenkel (1976), Dornbusch (1976), Bilson (1978), Frankel (1979) and Hooper and Morton (1982) are the main references to the literature on monetary models of exchange rate determination.

Meese and Rogoff (1983) tested those models of exchange rate determination by means of a prediction exercise that compared their forecasting ability. They examined three bilateral US$ exchange rates *vis a vis* the British pound, German mark and Japanese yen and a trade-weighted exchange rate. Their comparison also included the simple random walk model, some univariate time series models, the forward rate as well as a VAR system. Their findings were quite discouraging from a theoretical point of view since none of the structural monetary models was able to outperform the naive random walk model[1]. This empirical regularity is more surprising than might appear at first sight since the forecasts generated by the structural models were based on actual values of the explanatory variables. Meese and Rogoff's work gave rise to a growing body of literature on the subject of nominal exchange rate prediction.

Some authors enhanced the static structural monetary models by

---

1 In fact the random walk performed better than any of the models considered, including the time series models.

including lagged variables to allow for dynamic adjustment[2]. Somanath (1986) nested the structural models for the German mark and the random walk in dynamic specifications that appended a lagged value of the exchange rate to the list of regressors of structural models[3]. His results accord with Meese and Rogoff's, though when the sample period is enlarged the dynamic structural models slightly outperform the random walk[4]. Boothe and Glassman (1987) analyzed the German mark and Canadian dollar rates by including lagged values of the exchange rate as well as those of the explanatory variables of structural models. Their results confirm earlier findings that simple time series models such as the random walk rank highest in forecast accuracy.

On the other hand, more supportive evidence of the monetary model has been found when this is cast in a rational expectations framework. The *assets market view*[5] of exchange rate determination described in chapter 2 nests all these types of rational expectations models.

Finn (1986), studies a rational expectations monetary model for the British pound rate. The predictions of her structural-rational expectations model, when estimated by FIML, are closer to those of the

---

2 Meese and Rogoff (1983) also compare the forecasting ability of dynamic structural models, but they do not report their results.

3 Thus, the models he estimates are linear combinations of structural models and the random walk.

4 It is necessary to point out that Somanath does not consider the pure random walk model but an AR(1).

5 Frenkel and Mussa (1985).

random walk than those of the pure structural models estimated by instrumental variables. Woo (1985) implements the rational expectations version of the monetary model specifying money demand functions for the US$ and German mark that allow for partial adjustment. His findings are quite impressive, the exchange rate predictions of his model outperform the random walk at all prediction horizons[6]. Wolff (1988) studies the same bilateral exchange rates as Meese and Rogoff in the light of the rational expectations assumption. The random walk slightly improves the forecasting performance of his model.

Other prediction exercises have tried to improve exchange rate forecasts by allowing for nonlinearities in two different ways. One possible way of capturing those nonlinearities is by means of time varying parameters. Schinasi and Swamy (1989) consider fixed and variable coefficients versions of traditional structural models for the pound, mark, and yen dollar rates using Meese and Rogoff's data set. They include a lagged dependent variable in both kind of models which makes a substantial difference in the forecasting ability of all structural models under study. Multistep-ahead forecasts of the stochastic coefficient versions of the structural models with lagged dependent variable, proved to be more accurate than one-step-ahead forecasts of the random walk model. However, they use actual values of the contemporaneous explanatory variables and do not perform sequential estimation in order to compute the measures of forecast accuracy.

In the same spirit, but using a Bayesian time varying

---

6 Woo (1983) does not say whether he uses the estimated random walk or not.

coefficient autoregressive model (TVC), Canova (1990) approaches the problem of forecasting exchange rates. The TVC model he proposes includes as special cases a great variety of parametric nonlinear models, and he shows that if it is used as the data generating model it produces nonlinearities and nonnormalities that have been detected in the conditional moments of asset prices, and particularly in exchange rates. He uses weekly data on five different dollar rates (French and Swiss franc, German mark, English pound, and Japanese Yen) as well as short term interest rates on eurodeposits denominated in those currencies and considers them as a system in the forecasting exercise exploiting their possible common features. Using the usual criteria for comparison of forecasting performance the TVC model improves the random walk forecasts. This improvement is of a higher order for the 13 steps horizon than for 1-step ahead, leading to the conclusion that nonlinearities become important primarily in the long run so that the forecasting performance of the TVC model is better for long horizons.

Another way of accounting for nonlinearities to improve forecasts has been the use of nonparametric estimation. In this direction are the works of Diebold and Nason (1990) and Mizrach (1990). The first study nonparametrically estimates the conditional mean functions of ten major weekly nominal dollar spot rates, from 1973 to 1987, and uses them to forecast in-sample and out-of-sample. By doing so, they avoid the parametric model-selection problem, since the number of parametric nonlinear models that can be plausible nonlinear DGP's is quite big. Diebold and Nason use as estimation method a generalized nearest-neighbor (NN) technique, known as locally weighted regression. They are interested in percent rate changes to avoid problems of nonstationarity in nonparametric estimation. Using that technique they estimate nonparametric autoregressions of different orders and examine the in-sample fit and out-sample predictive performance of their estimator. Their results depend on the choice of a smoothing parameter, so they choose an optimal one in terms of minimizing the mean squared prediction error (MSE) and the mean absolute prediction error (MAE). For the case of in-sample analysis, the one-step ahead MSE and MAE associated with the optimal choice of the smoothing parameter are always smaller than those of the random walk. On the contrary, the out-of-sample performance is not as good as the in-sample. For one-step-ahead the random walk turns out to be much better and out-of-sample loss reductions due to the use of nonparametric estimation generally do not exist. The results for 4, 8, and 12 step-ahead forecast are similar. This finding contrasts with the one obtained by Canova (1990) as commented above.

The second study, by Mizrach, uses the same statistical technique though he incorporates structural information into the nonparametric analysis by using a multivariate approach. He contemplates the close linkages of the currencies analyzed (French Franc, Italian Lira, and German mark) given the policy coordination of those countries as members of the European Monetary System. The nearest-neighbor technique is applied for different weight schemes and it is generalized for the multivariate case. As a benchmark, the random walk model is also included in the study. The data used is daily in sharp contrast with other studies, mostly using monthly or weekly data. For the univariate case, the use of the weighted NN regression gives the best forecasts and the MSE in that case are very close to those for the random walk, being outperformed in the case of the Lira. The multivariate results show a great improvement over the univariate ones. In any case, the random walk is beaten just in the case of the Lira again. A cross-validation exercise puts into question the robustness of this result.

Finally, another approach to exchange rate prediction is that employed by Engel and Hamilton (1990). They have used a model of regime switching to account for exchange rate movements. The rate of growth of the exchange rate[7] of three US$ exchange rates (*vis a vis* the french franc, german mark and british pound over the period 1973-87 using quarterly rates) are assumed to be generated by a two-state stochastic segmented trends model. That is, ε_t is drawn either from a $N(\mu_1,\sigma_1^2)$ distribution if the latent variable $I_t = 1$ or from a $N(\mu_2,\sigma_2^2)$ distribution if the latent variable $I_t = 2$. The model captures very well the long up and down swings of the dollar rates analyzed. The forecasts generated by this model beat a random walk with fitted drift at the 1, 2, 3 and 4 quarters horizons (both in-sample and out-sample). However, the naive driftless random walk outperforms the stochastic segmented trends forecasts in terms of MSE.

III. Forecasting Exercise

The three exchange rate systems described in chapter 4 were estimated under five different scenarios:

(i) Unrestricted model.

(ii) Restricted short run dynamics.

(iii) Restricted long run dynamics.

(iv) Restricted short and long run dynamics.

---

7 i.e. $\varepsilon_t = s_t - s_{t-1}$ where $s_t = \log(S_t)$ and S_t is the spot rate.

(v) VAR in first differences ⇒ No cointegration.

The first four scenarios correspond to the cases analyzed in chapter 7.

The models (i)-(v) were first estimated for the sample period April 1973 to March 1986 and used to generate 1 to 36 step-ahead forecasts based on the available information up to March 1986. Then an additional observation was included and the models were reestimated and used for prediction again. This process was repeated up until the end of the sample. Finally, mean squared, root mean squared and absolute mean squared forecast errors as well as Theil's U statistics were calculated. All the discussion below refers to the forecasts generated by the exchange rate equations.

Table I reports those statistics for the three unrestricted VAR (scenario (i)). In no case the unrestricted VAR has a U statistic smaller than unity, meaning that the naive random walk predicts better at any step.

As a second specification we allow for different lag length in the equations of the VAR. One of the reasons to do that is because for some bilateral systems it is not possible to obtain white noise residuals in all the equations simultaneously for a common lag length. Another reason is that it may save a lot of parameters because some equations, in particular the exchange rate equation, do not require a lag length as large as others, e.g. the interest rates equations. The Ljung-Box Q statistic was used once again in order to determine the lag length at which the residuals from each of the equations were serially uncorrelated. Once the set of regressors in each equation is different, efficiency can be improved if the SURE estimator is used. We estimated the three systems in their ECM[8] form using the SURE technique and used the t-stat from those regressions in order to exclude the regressors whose coefficients were not significantly different from zero[9]. After imposing the zero restrictions the three systems were estimated by SURE and used for prediction. Table II summarizes the statistics of forecast accuracy using both OLS and GLS for the exchange rate equations of the three systems (scenario (ii)). Comparing the forecasting performance of the unrestricted model with the restricted one estimated by OLS, we observe an improvement in the short term forecast horizons for all three systems that worsens for the cases of Germany / US and UK / US as the forecasting horizon increases. The improvement is maintained at all horizons in the Japan / US system. The random walk is beaten in the case of the mark / $ rate at 1, 3 and 6 steps ahead and in the case of the yen / $ rate at 6 and 12. The same comments apply to the case when SURE was used to estimate the model. We observe no gain, sometimes even loss, in terms of prediction accuracy compared with OLS.

Next, the three VAR systems were estimated imposing the long run restrictions implied by cointegration. The estimation method is that outlined in section 7.III developed by Johansen. For this purpose, all

---

8 Those ECM were not subject to the long-run restriction $\Pi=\alpha\beta'$.

9 Because the regressions involve several lags of the same variables multicollinearity is expected to appear and therefore it should bc taken into account in using the t-stats. Note that the asymptotic distribution of the t-stat is standard only for the stationary regressors and not for the levels and the deterministic terms.

equations were assumed to have the same lag length and no zero restrictions were imposed on the short run parameters, so that the short run dynamics were not restricted. Likelihood ratio tests for the number of cointegrating vectors were reported in chapter 4. The estimated systems were used to generate forecasts of all the variables and table III reports the statistics for the three US$ exchange rates forecasts (scenario (iii)). The German / US system under long run restrictions predicts better than the unrestricted system at all horizons. However, the same system with only short run restrictions predicts better for short lead forecasts. The Japan / US is the system with largest number of cointegrating vectors, and therefore very close to the unrestricted estimated VAR. There is almost no improvement with respect to the unrestricted case. Furthermore, the predictions are worse at the 36th step-ahead horizon. The results are worse at all horizons than those obtained with the short run dynamics restricted. Finally, the UK / US system benefits from the cointegrating restrictions for the case of 12, 24 and 36 steps ahead, with respect to the unrestricted and the short-run restricted cases. Only in the case of the Germany / US system, the long run restrictions help outperforming the random walk.

Some of the cointegrating vectors might have little bearing in exchange rate determination. In terms of the ECM, this would show up as zero restrictions on the elements of the first row of the loadings matrix α. We have generated predictions with some of those restrictions imposed and they are summarized in table IV[10]. The restrictions on the

---

10 The restrictions on α_1 were imposed only for prediction, not for estimation.

first row of the loadings matrix improve the forecasting performance of the models with respect to the previous scenario except for the 36 step horizon in the UK / US system.

Using the two-step procedure explained in (7.III.2) we estimated the models under both zero restrictions on the short run parameters and also the restrictions given by cointegration (scenario (iv)). The results are reported in table V. When compared with scenario (i), the UK / US system shows an improvement at all steps, the Japan / US worsens at all steps and the Germany / US system presents an improvement only at 1, 12, 24 36 steps. On the other hand, compared with scenario (iii), the predictions are in general better except for 1 step-ahead in the Japan / US case, 36 step-ahead in the UK / US and 6, 12, 24 and 36 steps ahead in the Germany / US case.

Finally, the predictions using a VAR in first differences are compared with all previous ones. The interesting point of using this specification for prediction is that if there is cointegration, the VAR in first differences is misspecified. It imposes more unit roots than there are because it is a fully nonstationary model. Table VI reports the results for the VAR in first differences. Overall, its performance is very good. For all three systems it outperforms the unrestricted VAR at all steps except for the UK / US system at 1 and 3 steps ahead. The VAR in first differences does better than the long run restricted ECM for the cases of Germany and Japan at any horizon but not in the case of the UK / US system with 8 unit roots imposed.

We can think of some possible explanations for this outcome. On the one hand, the exchange rate could be weakly exogenous with respect to the cointegrating vectors, so that the first row of the loadings matrix α_1 would be zero[11]. In such a case the equilibrium error would not play any role in the short run dynamics of the exchange rate.

On the other hand, the results of a simulation exercise that we will analyze in chapter 4 point towards the same direction as this prediction exercise. The VAR in first differences seems to be the strongest adversary, specially when some of the variables are weakly exogenous and the system is closer to the fully nonstationary case.

Next we turn to the analysis of the prediction bias by comparing the mean errors. The VAR in first differences is a misspecified model and therefore the OLS estimator of this model should have a misspecification bias. This in turn ought to be reflected in terms of prediction bias. However, the VAR in first differences has smaller mean errors (in absolute terms) than the unrestricted and long run restricted models for several forecast horizons.

IV. Conclusions

In this chapter we have used a multivariate time series model in order to predict three US$ nominal exchange rates. The exchange rate and some observable fundamentals are cast in a VAR. From a theoretical point of view this specification is consistent with structural models of exchange rate determination. From a statistical one, it allows for nonstationarity and cointegration. The forecasting exercise compares prediction accuracy among several specifications. Only in the case of the mark / dollar rate the predictions of the models fitted outperformed

---

11 In chapter 5, we found the exchange rate weakly exogenous.

the random walk at some horizons. Overall, the VAR in first differences predicts the exchange rate better than the other models considered.

APPENDIX A

SOME DEFINITIONS

$$\text{MEAN ERROR} = \sum_{t=T}^{T+N_h} (x_{t+h} - f_{t+h}) / N_h$$

$$\text{MEAN ABSOLUTE ERROR} = \sum_{t=T}^{T+N_h} |x_{t+h} - f_{t+h}| / N_h$$

$$\text{ROOT MEAN SQUARED ERROR} = \left(\sum_{t=T}^{T+N_h} (x_{t+h} - f_{t+h})^2 / N_h \right)^{1/2}$$

THEIL's U = ROOT MEAN SQUARED ERROR / ROOT MEAN SQUARED ERROR of random walk.

N. OBS. = Number of h-step ahead forecasts computed = N_h.

h = number of steps ahead. t = end of estimation period. x_{t+h} = actual value.

f_{t+h} = h step ahead forecast generated with model estimated up until period t.

Table I. Unrestricted VAR predictions.

STEP	MEAN ERROR	MEAN ABS. ERROR	RMS ERROR	THEIL U	N. OBS.
		Germany / US.			
1	-0.3219E-02	0.3340E-01	0.4114E-01	1.1554	48
3	-0.1210E-01	0.6273E-01	0.7960E-01	1.2230	46
6	-0.1016E-01	0.9546E-01	0.1107	1.1793	43
12	0.3393E-01	0.1365	0.1626	1.4051	37
24	0.1118	0.2365	0.2642	2.0392	25
36	-0.5194E-01	0.1511	0.1869	1.5897	13
		Japan / US			
1	-0.3013E-02	0.3221E-01	0.3967E-01	1.0878	48
3	-0.1003E-01	0.6535E-01	0.8183E-01	1.2877	46
6	-0.1183E-01	0.8596E-01	0.1140	1.3458	43
12	-0.8481E-02	0.1277	0.1693	1.3314	37
24	0.4690E-01	0.2265	0.2594	1.4238	25
36	0.3158E-01	0.2168	0.2752	1.8584	13
		UK / US			
1	-0.4051E-02	0.3471E-01	0.3979E-01	1.1251	48
3	-0.3624E-02	0.6021E-01	0.7549E-01	1.2232	46
6	0.1614E-01	0.8750E-01	0.1046	1.2964	43
12	0.5537E-01	0.1668	0.1907	1.7467	37
24	0.1732E-01	0.2927	0.3374	2.3955	25
36	-0.3335	0.3335	0.3408	3.8206	13

Table II. Restricted Short Run Dynamics.

STEP	MEAN ERROR	MEAN ABS. ERROR	RMS ERROR	THEIL U
		Germany / US. OLS.		
1	-0.7962E-03	0.2884E-01	0.3506E-01	0.9848
3	-0.2348E-02	0.4956E-01	0.6143E-01	0.9438
6	-0.8188E-02	0.7778E-01	0.9321E-01	0.9925
12	-0.2099E-01	0.1328	0.1623	1.4021
24	-0.3048E-01	0.2315	0.2704	2.0872
36	-0.2496	0.2861	0.3253	2.7666
		Germany / US. SURE.		
1	-0.7962E-03	0.2884E-01	0.3506E-01	0.9848
3	-0.2370E-02	0.4935E-01	0.6105E-01	0.9381
6	-0.8451E-02	0.7575E-01	0.9106E-01	0.9697
12	-0.1993E-01	0.1296	0.1581	1.3655
24	-0.1882E-01	0.2323	0.2684	2.0716
36	-0.2271	0.2838	0.3179	2.7039

Table II. Restricted Short Run Dynamics. (Continued.)

STEP	MEAN ERROR	MEAN ABS. ERROR	RMS ERROR	THEIL U
		Japan / US. OLS.		
1	0.7912E-02	0.3182E-01	0.3724E-01	1.0211
3	0.2188E-01	0.5631E-01	0.6554E-01	1.0313
6	0.3911E-01	0.7039E-01	0.8400E-01	0.9911
12	0.4789E-01	0.1014	0.1190	0.9359
24	0.4753E-01	0.1696	0.2001	1.0984
36	0.3312E-01	0.1278	0.1594	1.0768
		Japan / US. SURE.		
1	0.7912E-02	0.3182E-01	0.3724E-01	1.0211
3	0.2193E-01	0.5619E-01	0.6544E-01	1.0297
6	0.3926E-01	0.6992E-01	0.8357E-01	0.9860
12	0.5034E-01	0.1013	0.1191	0.9368
24	0.5442E-01	0.1729	0.2022	1.1098
36	0.3941E-01	0.1326	0.1666	1.1249

STEP	MEAN ERROR	MEAN ABS. ERROR	RMS ERROR	THEIL U
		UK / US. OLS.		
1	0.2322E-02	0.3051E-01	0.3642E-01	1.0300
3	0.5244E-02	0.5279E-01	0.6409E-01	1.0385
6	0.6961E-02	0.8093E-01	0.9989E-01	1.2369
12	-0.7684E-02	0.1657	0.1833	1.6794
24	-0.1069	0.2765	0.3089	2.1936
36	-0.3676	0.3676	0.3722	4.1730
		UK / US. SURE.		
1	0.2317E-02	0.3051E-01	0.3643E-01	1.0301
3	0.5129E-02	0.5277E-01	0.6407E-01	1.0381
6	0.6533E-02	0.8111E-01	0.1000	1.2386
12	-0.8637E-02	0.1668	0.1846	1.6914
24	-0.1131	0.2818	0.3140	2.2299
36	-0.3768	0.3768	0.3816	4.2785

Table III. Restricted Long Run Dynamics.

STEP	MEAN ERROR	MEAN ABS. ERROR	RMS ERROR	THEIL U
		Germany / US. r = 2.		
1	-0.1639E-03	0.3094E-01	0.3754E-01	1.0545
3	-0.4034E-02	0.5476E-01	0.6623E-01	1.0176
6	-0.4638E-02	0.7747E-01	0.9286E-01	0.9888
12	0.1908E-01	0.1015	0.1250	1.0804
24	0.6050E-01	0.1449	0.1663	1.2840
36	-0.2204E-01	0.5645E-01	0.6877E-01	0.5847
		Germany / US. r = 3.		
1	0.1286E-02	0.3156E-01	0.3810E-01	1.0701
3	-0.5831E-03	0.5618E-01	0.6729E-01	1.0340
6	0.5051E-04	0.7579E-01	0.9149E-01	0.9742
12	0.3034E-01	0.9600E-01	0.1197	1.0345
24	0.9314E-01	0.1495	0.1693	1.3071
36	0.4667E-01	0.8696E-01	0.1049	0.8920

STEP	MEAN ERROR	MEAN ABS. ERROR	RMS ERROR	THEIL U
		Japan / US. r = 5.		
1	-0.1421E-02	0.3171E-01	0.3861E-01	1.0587
3	-0.3068E-02	0.6351E-01	0.7770E-01	1.2227
6	0.3572E-02	0.8184E-01	0.1025	1.2102
12	0.3028E-01	0.1156	0.1398	1.0996
24	0.1018	0.2097	0.2346	1.2875
36	0.1830	0.2891	0.3235	2.1846
		Japan / US. r = 6.		
1	-0.2276E-02	0.3219E-01	0.3934E-01	1.0788
3	-0.7355E-02	0.6611E-01	0.8100E-01	1.2746
6	-0.1686E-02	0.8832E-01	0.1109	1.3085
12	0.1705E-01	0.1246	0.1526	1.2003
24	0.7630E-01	0.2015	0.2266	1.2440
36	0.1355	0.2468	0.2834	1.9135

Table III. Restricted Long Run Dynamics. (Continued.)

STEP	MEAN ERROR	MEAN ABS. ERROR	RMS ERROR	THEIL U
		UK / US. r = 1.		
1	-0.9476E-02	0.3431E-01	0.4124E-01	1.1663
3	-0.2453E-01	0.6309E-01	0.7869E-01	1.2750
6	-0.3746E-01	0.7385E-01	0.9747E-01	1.2070
12	-0.5646E-01	0.1005	0.1209	1.1080
24	-0.1221	0.1435	0.1764	1.2529
36	-0.1669	0.1669	0.1741	1.9524
		UK / US. r = 3.		
1	-0.9102E-02	0.3467E-01	0.4121E-01	1.1652
3	-0.1873E-01	0.6351E-01	0.7958E-01	1.2894
6	-0.1191E-01	0.7747E-01	0.9801E-01	1.2137
12	0.1698E-01	0.1030	0.1284	1.1765
24	0.5672E-01	0.1747	0.2206	1.5663
36	0.2590E-01	0.1089	0.1361	1.5265

Table IV. Restricted Long Run Dynamics and Loadings Matrix.

STEP	MEAN ERROR	MEAN ABS. ERROR	RMS ERROR	THEIL U
	Germany / US. $r = 2.$ $\alpha_{12} = 0.$			
1	-0.1975E-04	0.3048E-01	0.3733E-01	1.0484
3	-0.3957E-02	0.5330E-01	0.6470E-01	0.9942
6	-0.5083E-02	0.7451E-01	0.8937E-01	0.9516
12	0.1676E-01	0.9678E-01	0.1183	1.0225
24	0.5480E-01	0.1321	0.1502	1.1598
36	-0.1613E-01	0.5113E-01	0.6457E-01	0.5491
	Germany / US. $r = 3.$ $\alpha_{12} = 0,$ $\alpha_{13} = 0.$			
1	-0.1975E-04	0.3048E-01	0.3733E-01	1.0484
3	-0.4269E-02	0.5262E-01	0.6400E-01	0.9834
6	-0.6319E-02	0.6984E-01	0.8489E-01	0.9039
12	0.2017E-01	0.8728E-01	0.1080	0.9333
24	0.7749E-01	0.1259	0.1400	1.0809
36	0.4681E-01	0.7236E-01	0.9612E-01	0.8173

STEP	MEAN ERROR	MEAN ABS. ERROR	RMS ERROR	THEIL U
	Japan / US. $r = 5.$ $\alpha_{12} = \alpha_{13} = \alpha_{14} = \alpha_{15} = 0.$			
1	-0.1487E-02	0.3147E-01	0.3780E-01	1.0365
3	-0.3905E-02	0.5956E-01	0.7246E-01	1.1402
6	0.2562E-02	0.7702E-01	0.9449E-01	1.1148
12	0.2438E-01	0.1086	0.1317	1.0357
24	0.9181E-01	0.1916	0.2121	1.1644
36	0.1738	0.2616	0.2939	1.9846
	Japan / US. $r = 5.$ $\alpha_{11} = \alpha_{13} = \alpha_{14} = \alpha_{15} = 0.$			
1	-0.1487E-02	0.3147E-01	0.3780E-01	1.0365
3	-0.5906E-02	0.5953E-01	0.7300E-01	1.1486
6	0.2964E-02	0.7881E-01	0.9610E-01	1.1338
12	0.2328E-01	0.1131	0.1373	1.0802
24	0.7460E-01	0.1879	0.2094	1.1496
36	0.1422	0.2295	0.2636	1.7802

Table IV. Restricted Long Run Dynamics and Loadings Matrix. (Cont'd)

STEP	MEAN ERROR	MEAN ABS. ERROR	RMS ERROR	THEIL U
		UK. / US. r = 3. $\alpha_{12} = 0$, $\alpha_{13} = 0$.		
1	-0.9476E-02	0.3431E-01	0.4124E-01	1.1663
3	-0.1990E-01	0.6334E-01	0.7888E-01	1.2781
6	-0.1412E-01	0.7561E-01	0.9397E-01	1.1636
12	0.1131E-01	0.8266E-01	0.1032	0.9451
24	0.5342E-01	0.1368	0.1608	1.1422
36	0.1085	0.1445	0.1991	2.2328
		UK. / US. r = 3. $\alpha_{11} = 0$, $\alpha_{13} = 0$.		
1	-0.6133E-02	0.3387E-01	0.3991E-01	1.1286
3	-0.1112E-01	0.6014E-01	0.7420E-01	1.2023
6	-0.2466E-02	0.7395E-01	0.9191E-01	1.1381
12	0.2774E-01	0.8350E-01	0.1068	0.9781
24	0.8153E-01	0.1484	0.1757	1.2480
36	0.1262	0.1456	0.1961	2.1987

Table V. Restricted Short and Long Run Dynamics.

STEP	MEAN ERROR	MEAN ABS. ERROR	RMS ERROR	THEIL U
		Germany / US. r = 3.		
1	-2.9521E-03	2.9377E-02	3.5037E-02	0.97369
3	-8.5508E-03	5.2798E-02	6.4095E-02	0.97405
6	-1.1239E-02	8.0496E-02	9.4105E-02	0.99035
12	1.9844E-03	1.0594E-01	1.2909E-01	1.0998
24	4.4955E-02	1.5622E-01	1.7434E-01	1.3184
36	-2.8241E-02	9.9274E-02	1.1151E-01	0.91098
		Japan / US. r = 6.		
1	1.0488E-02	3.2420E-02	3.7179E-02	1.10087
3	3.2739E-02	5.7403E-02	6.8397E-02	1.10645
6	7.1317E-02	8.6358E-02	1.0164E-01	1.11852
12	1.5333E-01	1.6500E-01	1.8052E-01	1.14003
24	3.4242E-01	3.5238E-01	3.8700E-01	1.20809
36	5.0515E-01	5.0515E-01	5.3722E-01	1.34848
		UK / US. r = 3.		
1	-4.9557E-03	2.9832E-02	3.5893E-02	1.0043
3	-1.6455E-02	5.2541E-02	6.1945E-02	0.9927
6	-3.5939E-02	6.5756E-02	8.3752E-02	1.0250
12	-9.6373E-02	1.1725E-01	1.4202E-01	1.2829
24	-2.2443E-01	2.2748E-01	2.6655E-01	1.8542
36	-3.8246E-01	3.8246E-01	3.7253E-01	4.0125

Table VI. VAR in First Differences.

STEP	MEAN ERROR	MEAN ABS. ERROR	RMS ERROR	THEIL U
		Germany / US.		
1	-0.1126E-03	0.3036E-01	0.3698E-01	1.0385
3	-0.4705E-02	0.5230E-01	0.6324E-01	0.9717
6	-0.9423E-02	0.7353E-01	0.8689E-01	0.9253
12	0.4602E-02	0.8286E-01	0.1050	0.9071
24	0.2605E-01	0.1083	0.1293	0.9981
36	-0.1356E-01	0.5307E-01	0.6533E-01	0.5555
		Japan / US		
1	0.1434E-02	0.3248E-01	0.3842E-01	1.0536
3	0.6060E-02	0.5924E-01	0.7121E-01	1.1205
6	0.1006E-01	0.7325E-01	0.8939E-01	1.0546
12	0.1187E-01	0.1042	0.1201	0.9449
24	0.1980E-01	0.1455	0.1796	0.9857
36	0.4449E-01	0.1373	0.1555	1.0501
		UK / US		
1	-0.4592E-02	0.3586E-01	0.4098E-01	1.1588
3	-0.1060E-01	0.6245E-01	0.7758E-01	1.2570
6	-0.1694E-01	0.7399E-01	0.9608E-01	1.1898
12	-0.3939E-01	0.1028	0.1234	1.1307
24	-0.1089	0.1493	0.1790	1.2708
36	-0.1693	0.1693	0.1765	1.9791

Chapter 10. A Simulation Exercise

I. Introduction

Engle and Yoo (1987) use a small simulation exercise to compare the forecasting ability of a bivariate unrestricted VAR including just one lag with that of an ECM estimated by the two-step procedure proposed by Engle and Granger (1987). The restricted ECM outperforms, in terms of mean squared error, its unrestricted opponent if the number of steps ahead predicted is six or greater. They argue that the better performance of the unrestricted VAR in the short run might be due to the long run character of the constraints. Hence, according to their argument, the restricted ECM would be misspecified in the short run. Whereas, it would be correctly specified once the forecasting horizon were such that the cointegrating restrictions became true.

We agree with Engle and Yoo in that better forecasts will be obtained if the restrictions implied by cointegration are imposed at the estimation stage with respect to the case when those restrictions are not imposed. An unrestricted VAR in levels would not incorporate all available information and thus generate worse predictions, specially as the forecasting horizon increases. The estimated unrestricted long run impact matrix Π, though close, will not be of reduced rank but of full rank. Ahn and Reinsel (1990) argue that because the full rank least squares estimates correspond to a fully stationary model, its forecasts are driven to the estimated mean value of the series as the lead time increases. On the other hand, imposing the reduced rank restriction will explicitly incorporate the unit roots or common trends that characterize the vector process.

On the other hand, we do not believe in their explanation for the better short-run forecasting performance of the unrestricted VAR. The reason why the unrestricted VAR in levels outperforms the restricted one for short-term horizons is because of the estimation method they use and the specific parameter values chosen. The restrictions on Π are satisfied regardless of the forecasting horizon, but when we estimate the restricted Π we make some estimation error for finite samples. In their case, this error resulted in a better predictive performance of the unrestricted VAR compared with the ECM estimated by the Engle and Granger procedure.

One of the motivations for the simulation is, therefore, to analyze whether the use of other methods of estimation and parameter values of the DGP, will result in a different conclusion. In particular we use Johansen's (1988b) method.

Moreover, they also conclude that[1]:

> "One could also compare these results with estimates which are obviously misspecified such as least squares on differences or Litterman's (1986) Bayesian Vector Autoregression which shrinks the parameter vector towards the first difference model which is itself misspecified for this system. The finding that such methods provided inferior forecasts would hardly be surprising."

Contrary to what Engle and Yoo assume not to be surprising, we show below, by means of a simulation exercise, that a VAR in first differences, even though it is misspecified, generates in many cases

---

1 Engle and Yoo (1987) pp. 151-152.

better forecasts than the ECM estimated by Engle and Granger's or Johansen's procedures.

Another interesting feature of the simulation exercise is that, it allows us to compare the forecasting accuracy of the VAR in levels, which is correctly specified, with that of the VAR in first differences which is misspecified.

We use the simulation experiment for two purposes:

(a) On the one hand, we examine the relative forecasting accuracy of a cointegrated time series model estimated by the following methods:

(i) VAR in levels estimated by multivariate OLS. (VARL).

(ii) ECM estimated by Engle and Granger's procedure. (EG2).

(iii) ECM estimated by Johansen's FIML procedure. (JOHA).

(iv) VAR in first differences estimated by OLS. (VARD).

Note that the number of unit roots imposed in these estimation procedures is different. (i) assumes that there are no unit roots (underdifferencing), (ii) and (iii) assume a number of unit roots less than the dimension of the system and finally (iv) assumes the number of unit roots be equal to the number of variables in the system (overdifferencing).

To measure the forecasting accuracy of the predictions from (i)-(iv) we use the trace of the mean squared error matrix,

$$V(h) = E \{ (X_{t+h} - \hat{f}_{t+h})(X_{t+h} - \hat{f}_{t+h})' \}. \qquad (I.2)$$

Note that if $V(h) \geq B(h)$ then $tr(V(h)) \geq tr(B(h))$, but the opposite is not true. The determinant of $V(h)$ has been used in the preliminary analysis. As h grew, this measure wandered a lot, not allowing us to clearly compare the forecasting performance of the different models.

Thus, we decided not to include that measure in the report of the results.

(b) On the other hand, we use the simulated forecasts to determine the forecasting horizon h for which the long run cointegrating relationship is approximately satisfied by the true forecast. In order to do so we compute the following measure,

$$S(h) = (1/N) \sum_{i=1}^{N} (\beta' f^{i}_{t+h} - \beta' X_0)^2, \qquad (I.1)$$

where f^{i}_{t+h} is the true optimal h-step-ahead forecast at period t for the i-th replication and N is the number of replications. This measure is computed for different forecasting horizons.

II. The Data Generating Process

The data generating process (DGP) used is a slight modification of the one specified by Gonzalo (1989). We will consider the following design,

$$\begin{aligned} y_t - b\,x_t = z_t \quad &; \quad z_t = \rho_1 z_{t-1} + \rho_2 z_{t-2} + e_{z_t} \\ a\,y_t - c\,x_t = w_t \quad &; \quad w_t = w_{t-1} + e_{w_t} \end{aligned} \qquad (II.1)$$

$$\begin{bmatrix} e_{z_t} \\ e_{w_t} \end{bmatrix} \sim \text{IIN} \left\{ \begin{bmatrix} 0 \\ 0 \end{bmatrix} ; \begin{bmatrix} \sigma_w^2 & \delta\,\sigma_w \sigma_z \\ \delta\,\sigma_w \sigma_z & \sigma_z^2 \end{bmatrix} \right\}. \qquad (II.2)$$

We may write (II.1) in an structural Error Correction form as,

$$\begin{bmatrix} 1 & -b \\ a & -c \end{bmatrix} \begin{bmatrix} \Delta y_t \\ \Delta x_t \end{bmatrix} = \begin{bmatrix} \rho_1 + \rho_2 - 1 \\ 0 \end{bmatrix} z_{t-1} + \begin{bmatrix} -\rho_2 & \rho_2 b \\ 0 & 0 \end{bmatrix} \begin{bmatrix} \Delta y_{t-1} \\ \Delta x_{t-1} \end{bmatrix} + \begin{bmatrix} e_{z_t} \\ e_{w_t} \end{bmatrix}$$

The corresponding (reduced form) Error correction model is,

$$\begin{bmatrix} \Delta y_t \\ \Delta x_t \end{bmatrix} = \begin{bmatrix} \alpha_1 \\ \alpha_2 \end{bmatrix} z_{t-1} + \frac{1}{(ab-c)} \begin{bmatrix} \rho_2 c & \rho_2 bc \\ a\rho_2 & a\rho_2 b \end{bmatrix} \begin{bmatrix} \Delta y_{t-1} \\ \Delta x_{t-1} \end{bmatrix} + \begin{bmatrix} u_{1t} \\ u_{2t} \end{bmatrix}$$

$$\begin{bmatrix} u_{1t} \\ u_{2t} \end{bmatrix} \sim \text{IIN} \left\{ \begin{bmatrix} 0 \\ 0 \end{bmatrix} ; \begin{bmatrix} \sigma_1^2 & \sigma_{12} \\ \sigma_{12} & \sigma_2^2 \end{bmatrix} \right\} \tag{II.3}$$

or in more compact notation,

$$\Delta X_t = \alpha \beta' X_{t-1} + \Gamma_1 \Delta X_{t-1} + U_t, \tag{II.4}$$

where $\beta' = (1, -b)$. The parameters of this reduced form are expressed in terms of the structural form parameters as follows,

$$\alpha_1 = c(1 - \rho_1 - \rho_2)/\ (ab-c),\ \alpha_2 = a(1 - \rho_1 - \rho_2)/\ (ab-c), \tag{II.5}$$

$$\sigma_1^2 = [b^2\sigma_w^2 + c^2\sigma_z^2 - 2bc\delta\sigma_w\sigma_z] \ / \ (ab-c)^2,$$

$$\sigma_2^2 = [\sigma_w^2 + a^2\sigma_z^2 - 2a\delta\sigma_w\sigma_z] \ / \ (ab-c)^2,$$

$$\sigma_{12} = [b\sigma_w^2 - (ab+c)\delta\sigma_z\sigma_w + ac\sigma_z^2] \ / \ (ab-c)^2.$$

The (reduced form) VAR representation of this DGP is,

$$\begin{bmatrix} y_t \\ x_t \end{bmatrix} = \begin{bmatrix} (1+\alpha_1+\gamma_{11}) & (\gamma_{12}-\alpha_1 b) \\ (\alpha_2+\gamma_{21}) & (1-b\alpha_2+\gamma_{22}) \end{bmatrix} \begin{bmatrix} y_{t-1} \\ x_{t-1} \end{bmatrix} - \begin{bmatrix} \gamma_{11} & \gamma_{12} \\ \gamma_{21} & \gamma_{22} \end{bmatrix} \begin{bmatrix} y_{t-2} \\ x_{t-2} \end{bmatrix} + \begin{bmatrix} u_{1t} \\ u_{2t} \end{bmatrix}$$

or more compactly,

$$X_t = \Pi_1 X_{t-1} + \Pi_2 X_{t-2} + U_t, \qquad \text{(II.6)}$$

where $\Pi_2 = -\Gamma_1$. This will be the actual form of the DGP used in the simulation.

Let $\Pi(L) = I - \Pi_1 L - \Pi_2 L^2$ and assume that $|\Pi(1)| = 0$. Therefore, the vector X_t is not stationary but the first difference of X_t, ΔX_t, can be represented by a stationary infinite MA process.

On the other hand, there will be a linear combination $z_t = y_t - b\, x_t$ that is stationary, provided $\rho_1 + \rho_2 < 1$, $\rho_2 < 1 + \rho_1$ and $\rho_2 > -1$. The vector (1, -b) is called the cointegrating vector. If some of these three conditions are not satisfied, then there is no stationary linear combination between those variables.

The parameter space can be characterized by a vector $(a, b, c, \rho_1, \rho_2, \delta, \sigma_w^2, \sigma_z^2)'$ and a probability distribution for the disturbance term. We perform the simulations for $a = \{0, 1\}$, $\rho_1 = \{0.5, 0.9\}$, $\rho_2 = \{0, 0.05\}$, $b = 2$, $c = 0.5$, $\delta = \{0, 0.5\}$, $\sigma_1^2 = 1$, $\sigma_2^2 = \{1, 10\}$. These parameter values give rise to 32 different simulation experiments[2].

Given these parameter values, we have generated random drawings from a bivariate normal distribution with zero mean and covariance matrix (II.3). With these random disturbances and the reduced form (II.6) we have computed 136 values of x and y for each replication.

---

[2] We have also carried out simulations for the parameter values $b = -0.5$ and $\sigma_z^2 = 0.1$ giving rise to 128 simulations. However, we have decided not to report all the results since these parameter values add little to the picture described in the text.

The model is estimated using the first 100 observations, the initial conditions being zero. The 36 remaining observations are used for out-of-sample forecasting. For each set of parameter values this procedure is replicated 2,000 times.

III. Results

Appendix A reports, in tables 1 to 32, the ratio of the trace of the forecast error covariance matrix of a given model relative to that of a bivariate random walk. This is a way of normalizing the traces for comparison purposes, and can be considered as a multivariate version of Theil's U statistic. In addition the actual trace of the covariance matrix of the bivariate random walk forecast errors is also reported.

The simulation is divided in two parts concerning the lag structure of the DGP. When $\rho_2 = 0$, the VAR (II.6) becomes a first order one since $\Pi_2 = 0$. In this case the ECM has only the error correction term in the right hand side and the VAR in first differences becomes a bivariate random walk that requires no estimation. The simulations for this case are reported in tables 1 to 16 in appendix A of this chapter. It should be remarked that the results in this case will favor the bivariate random walk since the VARD does not incorporate any estimation error. For all these 16 cases we have also computed the measure (II.1).

On the other hand, when $\rho_2 = 0.05$, the DGP is a cointegrated second order VAR, the VAR in first differences has one lag and is estimated in the simulations. Tables 17 to 32 report simulations for this case in which all prediction methods incorporate some estimation error. This is a more fair comparison.

A close look to the results shows the relevance of different parameters and its interactions.

Let us consider the case when $\rho_2 = 0$. In this case, the parameter ρ_1 measures how close the cointegrated system is from a fully nonstationary system. As ρ_1 goes to one, the system converges to a bivariate random walk. In other words, as ρ_1 tends to unity, the error correction term enters the ECM with smaller weights. What we observe in the simulation is that for $\rho_1 = 0.9$, the EG2 and JOHA methods perform worse relative to VARD at all horizons than in the cases when $\rho_1 = 0.5$.

When $\rho_2 = 0.05$ the effect of ρ_1 on the forecasts is similar. The closer ρ_1 to unity the better VARD does, beating JOHA and EG2 at all horizons a greater number of times than when $\rho_2 = 0$. This is more surprising than before because in this case the VARD is estimated and therefore there is some estimation error involved.

The design of the simulation is such that for a = 0, the variable x_t is weakly exogenous with respect to β. If this is the case, the cointegrating residual does not enter the equation for x_t in the ECM. For a = 1, however, the error correction term enters both equations and therefore, imposing the cointegrating restrictions helps predicting both variables. This intuition is confirmed in the simulation. EG2 and JOHA do better for a = 1 than for a = 0 relative to the VARD.

The parameter σ_z^2 is the variance of the error term e_{z_t}. We have used three possible values of $\sigma_z^2 = \{0.1, 1, 10\}$ and report just those for $\sigma_z^2 = \{ 1, 10\}$. Given the specification chosen for z_t its variance is $[\sigma_z^2(1-\rho_2)/(1+\rho_2)((1-\rho_2)^2-\rho_1^2)]$. As σ_z^2 increases the magnitude of the error correction term rises and becomes more relevant. The result of the simulation show that the methods that take into account this error correction term (JOHA, EG2 and also VARL) benefit from a higher σ_z^2. The case $\sigma_z^2 = 0.1$ reinforces what we have said, i.e. the smaller σ_z^2, the better the VARD predicts.

The correlation coefficient of the structural disturbances, δ, plays an important role in the performance of EG2 and JOHA. While the JOHA procedure is robust to changes in δ, the EG2 performs much better when $\delta = 0$. When, in addition, a = 0, the structural system becomes a recursive one where estimation of the cointegrating regression (first equation) by OLS as in EG2 does not suffer from simultaneity bias. It is for some of these cases that EG2 beats JOHA. The VARD does much better when $\delta \neq 0$ than when $\delta = 0$, we cannot find an intuitive explanation for this.

Overall the VARL is a poor competitor. This is particularly interesting when compared with the VARD. Both estimated models impose an incorrect number of unit roots. However, overdifferencing is better than underdifferencing, at least in terms of forecasting performance. Underdifferencing yielded short run predictions that were better than the overdifferencing case when there were no weakly exogenous variables in the system (a = 1).

Regarding the speed with which the combination of forecasts $\beta' f_{t+h}$ converges towards its limit $\beta' X_0$ as h goes to infinity, the simulations show that the convergence is faster the farther away ρ_1 is from one and the greater σ_z^2 is. Many of the points of the parameter space that we have analyzed require only a short horizon (two or three steps ahead) in order for $\beta' f_{t+h}$ to become almost equal to $\beta' X_0$, that in the simulations is set equal to zero[3]. However, when $\rho_1 = 0.9$ we have to

---

[3] Since $X_0 = 0$, we are computing the measure,

$$S(h) = (1/2,000) \sum_{i=1}^{2000} (\beta' f^{i}_{t+h})^2.$$

allow h to go up to 20 or 30 in order to get the same degree of approximation as before. The error correction term becomes very important for points of the parameter space that would leave the system near the fully non-stationary case. Nevertheless, as we move towards those points, the weights of the error correction term in the ECM become closer to zero. Therefore, the results of this simulation favor the idea that the error correction term becomes less and less important as the forecasting horizon increases.

The main results of the simulation exercise are:

(i) The VARD, even though it is misspecified, generates better forecasts than the other estimated models, for parameter values such that the DGP is near to having a second unit root.

(ii) In those cases when the DGP is quite far from having two unit roots, the gain in predictive performance generated by imposing the cointegrating restrictions, with respect to the fully nonstationary model, is in many cases very small.

(iii) Whether the VARD is estimated or not makes little difference in the comparison of this with the other estimators. Moreover, when VARD is estimated performs better than when it is a nonestimated bivariate random walk.

(iv) In general, Johansen's estimation procedure yields estimated models that generate better predictions than the other estimation methods.

(v) The ECM estimated by Engle and Granger's two step procedure outperforms Johansen's method at some points of the parameter space, precisely those where there is no simultaneity bias.

(vi) The unrestricted VARL predicts, in some cases, better than the VARD and the EG2 in the short run.

Our results confirm what Reinsel and Ahn (1991) have pointed out, namely, that imposing more unit roots than the true number give longer term forecasts that perform better than the models with fewer unit roots imposed. Overall, the best performance corresponds to the model with the correct number of unit roots imposed.

Our results are not comparable with those of Davis and Newbold (1980). They carried out several simulation exercises where correctly specified univariate ARMA time series models were compared with misspecified pure autoregresive ones in terms of percentage losses in mean squared error. However, they do not fit the correctly specified model but rather use the true forecasts generated from that model. Nevertheless, our results agree with theirs in that as the forecast horizon increases, the difference in forecasting performance diminishes.

APPENDIX A

Tables 1 to 16 correspond to the case when $\rho_2 = 0$, and therefore the DGP is a first order cointegrated VAR. The estimated (misspecified) VAR in first differences corresponds to a bivariate random walk. In these tables we report the trace of the covariance matrix of prediction errors for the VARD (VAR in first differences). We report the multivariate Theil's U statistic defined in the main text. We also compute the measure S(h) (see chapter 10 section I) which gives an idea of how close is $\beta' f_{t+h}$ from being equal to $\beta' X_0$.

In tables 17 to 32, $\rho_2 \neq 0$ and the DGP is a second order cointegrated VAR. The estimated (misspecified) VAR in first differences corresponds in this case to a first order VAR. In these tables we report Theil's U statistic for all estimators.

Table 1.

$a = 0,\ b = 2,\ c = 0.5,\ \rho_1 = 0.5,\ \rho_2 = 0,\ \delta = 0,\ \sigma_w^2 = 1,\ \sigma_z^2 = 1.$

STEPS	EG2	JOHA	VARL	VARD	S(h)
1	1.0102	1.0058	1.0242	20.9650	0.33177
2	1.0066	0.9964	1.0315	41.7700	0.82943E-01
3	1.0035	1.0015	1.0510	63.1110	0.20736E-01
6	0.9941	0.9969	1.1278	120.7700	0.32400E-03
9	0.9947	0.9960	1.1763	186.3300	0.50624E-05
12	0.9995	0.9951	1.2214	255.2900	0.79101E-07
15	0.9985	0.9954	1.2800	317.5000	0.12359E-08
18	0.9984	0.9960	1.3528	370.3500	0.19312E-10
21	0.9973	0.9944	1.4253	427.9700	0.30174E-12
24	0.9968	0.9946	1.4953	483.8500	0.47148E-14
27	0.9975	0.9961	1.5670	550.1000	0.73668E-16
30	0.9978	0.9964	1.6402	621.4900	0.11511E-17
33	0.9978	0.9961	1.7404	696.1400	0.17985E-19
36	0.9989	0.9964	1.8400	752.0300	0.28102E-21

Table 2.

$a = 0,\ b = 2,\ c = 0.5,\ \rho_1 = 0.5,\ \rho_2 = 0,\ \delta = 0,\ \sigma_w^2 = 1,\ \sigma_z^2 = 10.$

STEPS	EG2	JOHA	VARL	VARD	S(h)
1	0.9528	0.9449	0.9571	31.9290	3.2051
2	0.9303	0.9183	0.9481	58.0840	0.80129
3	0.9276	0.9155	0.9631	82.7680	0.20032
6	0.9317	0.9296	1.0490	142.8500	0.31300E-02
9	0.9464	0.9425	1.1071	212.4400	0.48907E-04
12	0.9619	0.9566	1.1736	282.1700	0.76417E-06
15	0.9664	0.9614	1.2424	345.9500	0.11940E-07
18	0.9741	0.9699	1.3261	391.5200	0.18656E-09
21	0.9741	0.9711	1.3961	448.1900	0.29151E-11
24	0.9738	0.9713	1.4605	509.1700	0.45548E-13
27	0.9800	0.9767	1.5268	579.1300	0.71169E-15
30	0.9810	0.9765	1.5826	646.8000	0.11120E-16
33	0.9816	0.9771	1.6838	713.5600	0.17375E-18
36	0.9835	0.9796	1.7756	770.6500	0.27149E-20

Table 3.

a = 0, b = 2, c = 0.5, ρ_1 = 0.5, ρ_2 = 0, δ = 0.5, σ_w^2 = 1, σ_z^2 = 1.

STEPS	EG2	JOHA	VARL	VARD	S(h)
1	1.1792	0.9978	1.0159	17.1480	0.34661
2	1.2025	0.9889	1.0226	36.1170	0.86652E-01
3	1.1678	0.9975	1.0471	56.3930	0.21663E-01
6	1.1143	0.9960	1.1280	113.4700	0.33848E-03
9	1.0806	0.9959	1.1780	178.4300	0.52888E-05
12	1.0603	0.9954	1.2271	246.9100	0.82638E-07
15	1.0493	0.9956	1.2875	309.7400	0.12912E-08
18	1.0424	0.9965	1.3623	363.5400	0.20175E-10
21	1.0410	0.9945	1.4333	420.9700	0.31524E-12
24	1.0350	0.9953	1.5046	476.5200	0.49256E-14
27	1.0290	0.9968	1.5770	542.0800	0.76962E-16
30	1.0271	0.9976	1.6550	612.7300	0.12025E-17
33	1.0255	0.9977	1.7531	687.6500	0.18790E-19
36	1.0242	0.9973	1.8572	744.4700	0.29359E-21

Table 4.

a = 0, b = 2, c = 0.5, ρ_1 = 0.5, ρ_2 = 0, δ = 0.5, σ_w^2 = 1, σ_z^2 = 10.

STEPS	EG2	JOHA	VARL	VARD	S(h)
1	1.0112	0.8826	0.8919	19.8670	3.2930
2	1.0151	0.8533	0.8816	40.0880	0.82325
3	1.0160	0.8681	0.9169	61.1200	0.20581
6	1.0111	0.9075	1.0186	119.3300	0.32158E-02
9	1.0097	0.9322	1.0930	188.0500	0.50247E-04
12	1.0094	0.9491	1.1680	255.5800	0.78511E-06
15	1.0073	0.9573	1.2355	320.0800	0.12267E-07
18	1.0053	0.9664	1.3150	367.8000	0.19168E-09
21	1.0053	0.9681	1.3777	424.2900	0.29950E-11
24	1.0041	0.9708	1.4398	485.3200	0.46796E-13
27	1.0035	0.9762	1.4992	553.5800	0.73119E-15
30	1.0042	0.9765	1.5556	616.2400	0.11425E-16
33	1.0045	0.9759	1.6449	680.2800	0.17851E-18
36	1.0044	0.9775	1.7364	739.0700	0.27893E-20

Table 5.

$a = 0,\ b = 2,\ c = 0.5,\ \rho_1 = 0.9,\ \rho_2 = 0,\ \delta = 0,\ \sigma_w^2 = 1,\ \sigma_z^2 = 1.$

STEPS	EG2	JOHA	VARL	VARD	S(h)
1	1.0202	1.0222	1.0367	20.8580	4.5707
2	1.0360	1.0256	1.0536	41.8850	3.7023
3	1.0424	1.0399	1.0804	63.5560	2.9988
6	1.0478	1.0642	1.1681	122.6400	1.5937
9	1.0423	1.0783	1.2253	188.4900	0.84696
12	1.0443	1.0661	1.2557	257.8900	0.45011
15	1.0380	1.0672	1.3103	320.1300	0.23921
18	1.0293	1.0700	1.3695	374.7800	0.12712
21	1.0247	1.0759	1.4412	432.7800	0.67559E-01
24	1.0182	1.0776	1.5046	489.1100	0.35904E-01
27	1.0149	1.0865	1.5680	555.8300	0.19081E-01
30	1.0131	1.1000	1.6346	627.0700	0.10140E-01
33	1.0112	1.1168	1.7261	702.9800	0.53890E-02
36	1.0131	1.1301	1.8181	757.3100	0.28639E-02

Table 6.

$a = 0,\ b = 2,\ c = 0.5,\ \rho_1 = 0.9,\ \rho_2 = 0,\ \delta = 0,\ \sigma_w^2 = 1,\ \sigma_z^2 = 10.$

STEPS	EG2	JOHA	VARL	VARD	S(h)
1	1.0260	1.0195	1.0290	29.9780	44.970
2	1.0396	1.0223	1.0420	59.1260	36.426
3	1.0356	1.0213	1.0520	88.5140	29.505
6	1.0199	1.0257	1.1038	164.5300	15.680
9	0.9922	1.0256	1.1374	246.0000	8.3330
12	0.9810	1.0153	1.1679	327.2500	4.4285
15	0.9682	1.0091	1.2156	399.0700	2.3535
18	0.9633	1.0122	1.2767	454.1500	1.2507
21	0.9627	1.0162	1.3445	512.4100	0.66469
24	0.9545	1.0191	1.3976	577.9300	0.35325
27	0.9625	1.0287	1.4520	648.1900	0.18773
30	0.9680	1.0330	1.4986	719.8400	0.99767E-01
33	0.9679	1.0391	1.5767	795.7900	0.53020E-01
36	0.9749	1.0510	1.6633	844.7400	0.28177E-01

Table 7.

$a = 0,\ b = 2,\ c = 0.5,\ \rho_1 = 0.9,\ \rho_2 = 0,\ \delta = 0.5,\ \sigma_w^2 = 1,\ \sigma_z^2 = 1.$

STEPS	EG2	JOHA	VARL	VARD	S(h)
1	1.0402	1.0164	1.0339	16.9350	4.4892
2	1.0828	1.0200	1.0479	34.4070	3.6362
3	1.1019	1.0360	1.0834	52.7160	2.9454
6	1.1553	1.0542	1.1756	104.4800	1.5653
9	1.1556	1.0623	1.2366	163.7700	0.83186
12	1.1606	1.0524	1.2733	228.0200	0.44208
15	1.1540	1.0550	1.3366	287.5200	0.23494
18	1.1446	1.0617	1.4051	341.1700	0.12486
21	1.1309	1.0663	1.4783	397.9300	0.66354E-01
24	1.1225	1.0665	1.5464	452.6700	0.35263E-01
27	1.1144	1.0686	1.6105	518.2300	0.18740E-01
30	1.0990	1.0768	1.6899	587.4100	0.99594E-02
33	1.0945	1.0822	1.7831	661.4700	0.52928E-02
36	1.0893	1.0820	1.8844	717.9300	0.28128E-02

Table 8.

$a = 0,\ b = 2,\ c = 0.5,\ \rho_1 = 0.9,\ \rho_2 = 0,\ \delta = 0.5,\ \sigma_w^2 = 1,\ \sigma_z^2 = 10.$

STEPS	EG2	JOHA	VARL	VARD	S(h)
1	1.0213	1.0079	1.0180	17.5780	45.662
2	1.0383	1.0049	1.0269	35.4890	36.986
3	1.0448	0.9987	1.0370	54.1370	29.959
6	1.0643	0.9848	1.0733	107.0500	15.921
9	1.0613	0.9834	1.1116	167.5800	8.4612
12	1.0640	0.9733	1.1527	232.1700	4.4966
15	1.0576	0.9676	1.2029	295.1100	2.3897
18	1.0520	0.9728	1.2708	346.8800	1.2700
21	1.0471	0.9785	1.3389	401.3600	0.67492
24	1.0418	0.9836	1.3977	462.5300	0.35868
27	1.0385	0.9887	1.4490	529.3400	0.19062
30	1.0347	0.9943	1.5018	593.4300	0.10130
33	1.0323	0.9963	1.5750	662.1200	0.53836E-01
36	1.0292	1.0054	1.6601	716.7200	0.28611E-01

Table 9.

$a = 1,\ b = 2,\ c = 0.5,\ \rho_1 = 0.5,\ \rho_2 = 0,\ \delta = 0,\ \sigma_w^2 = 1,\ \sigma_z^2 = 1.$

STEPS	EG2	JOHA	VARL	VARD	S(h)
1	0.9467	0.9379	0.9435	3.0119	0.34588
2	0.9362	0.9361	0.9579	5.6388	0.86470E-01
3	0.9371	0.9438	0.9815	8.0877	0.21618E-01
6	0.9587	0.9625	1.0751	14.6070	0.33777E-03
9	0.9716	0.9732	1.1527	21.8520	0.52777E-05
12	0.9789	0.9764	1.1961	29.0210	0.82464E-07
15	0.9823	0.9819	1.2660	35.1000	0.12885E-08
18	0.9850	0.9866	1.3330	41.4200	0.20133E-10
21	0.9904	0.9914	1.4290	48.2160	0.31458E-12
24	0.9910	0.9918	1.5217	54.0360	0.49153E-14
27	0.9917	0.9937	1.6092	61.1680	0.76801E-16
30	0.9942	0.9963	1.7357	69.0040	0.12000E-17
33	0.9942	0.9971	1.8793	77.2050	0.18750E-19
36	0.9946	0.9963	2.0619	82.6080	0.29297E-21

Table 10.

$a = 1,\ b = 2,\ c = 0.5,\ \rho_1 = 0.5,\ \rho_2 = 0,\ \delta = 0,\ \sigma_w^2 = 1,\ \sigma_z^2 = 10.$

STEPS	EG2	JOHA	VARL	VARD	S(h)
1	0.9021	0.8138	0.8139	9.8241	3.4969
2	0.8757	0.7590	0.7656	15.7640	0.87422
3	0.8824	0.7341	0.7496	19.8190	0.21855
6	0.9226	0.7610	0.8122	27.7750	0.34149E-02
9	0.9361	0.8035	0.9012	35.7060	0.53358E-04
12	0.9367	0.8258	0.9734	42.3490	0.83372E-06
15	0.9506	0.8420	1.0406	47.4780	0.13027E-07
18	0.9583	0.8686	1.1288	54.1140	0.20354E-09
21	0.9712	0.8892	1.2321	61.0400	0.31804E-11
24	0.9732	0.8953	1.3133	67.0030	0.49693E-13
27	0.9841	0.9082	1.4079	73.5740	0.77646E-15
30	0.9827	0.9197	1.5388	81.8530	0.12132E-16
33	0.9872	0.9208	1.6622	89.4690	0.18957E-18
36	0.9844	0.9244	1.8075	93.6230	0.29620E-20

Table 11.

$a = 1,\ b = 2,\ c = 0.5,\ \rho_1 = 0.5,\ \rho_2 = 0,\ \delta = 0.5,\ \sigma_w^2 = 1,\ \sigma_z^2 = 1.$

STEPS	EG2	JOHA	VARL	VARD	S(h)
1	1.1503	0.8995	0.9040	2.1284	0.33063
2	1.1558	0.8960	0.9166	4.3399	0.82657E-01
3	1.1399	0.9116	0.9486	6.5569	0.20664E-01
6	1.0828	0.9478	1.0606	12.9370	0.32288E-03
9	1.0551	0.9669	1.1450	20.0790	0.50450E-05
12	1.0449	0.9730	1.1950	27.1700	0.78828E-07
15	1.0343	0.9805	1.2629	33.4260	0.12317E-08
18	1.0279	0.9831	1.3289	39.7970	0.19245E-10
21	1.0213	0.9883	1.4222	46.5660	0.30071E-12
24	1.0185	0.9901	1.5155	52.3500	0.46985E-14
27	1.0174	0.9900	1.5937	59.4570	0.73415E-16
30	1.0151	0.9928	1.7072	67.0590	0.11471E-17
33	1.0133	0.9946	1.8376	75.2180	0.17924E-19
36	1.0136	0.9935	1.9866	80.8810	0.28006E-21

Table 12.

$a = 1,\ b = 2,\ c = 0.5,\ \rho_1 = 0.5,\ \rho_2 = 0,\ \delta = 0.5,\ \sigma_w^2 = 1,\ \sigma_z^2 = 10.$

STEPS	EG2	JOHA	VARL	VARD	S(h)
1	0.8856	0.7227	0.7237	7.0897	3.4738
2	0.8507	0.6452	0.6488	11.7710	0.86846
3	0.8538	0.6313	0.6427	14.8860	0.21711
6	0.8829	0.6988	0.7402	22.2120	0.33924E-02
9	0.9096	0.7597	0.8484	30.1500	0.53006E-04
12	0.9275	0.7942	0.9431	36.5870	0.82822E-06
15	0.9363	0.8188	1.0259	42.0080	0.12941E-07
18	0.9437	0.8488	1.1268	48.6260	0.20220E-09
21	0.9527	0.8750	1.2325	55.6020	0.31594E-11
24	0.9577	0.8873	1.3308	61.2540	0.49366E-13
27	0.9640	0.8991	1.4356	68.1860	0.77134E-15
30	0.9693	0.9133	1.5813	75.3630	0.12052E-16
33	0.9702	0.9155	1.7273	82.3470	0.18832E-18
36	0.9712	0.9173	1.8943	87.0710	0.29425E-20

Table 13.

$a = 1,\ b = 2,\ c = 0.5,\ \rho_1 = 0.9,\ \rho_2 = 0,\ \delta = 0,\ \sigma_w^2 = 1,\ \sigma_z^2 = 1.$

STEPS	EG2	JOHA	VARL	VARD	S(h)
1	1.0091	1.0074	1.0118	2.8238	4.5001
2	1.0179	1.0080	1.0295	5.6474	3.6450
3	1.0198	1.0144	1.0536	8.4484	2.9525
6	1.0346	1.0235	1.1199	16.0310	1.5691
9	1.0314	1.0322	1.1811	24.3230	0.83387
12	1.0370	1.0199	1.2072	32.2670	0.44315
15	1.0322	1.0263	1.2628	39.0370	0.23551
18	1.0257	1.0309	1.3214	45.4520	0.12516
21	1.0246	1.0360	1.4024	52.4790	0.66515E-01
24	1.0193	1.0356	1.4911	58.4610	0.35349E-01
27	1.0221	1.0454	1.5898	65.5940	0.18786E-01
30	1.0202	1.0517	1.7136	73.8750	0.99835E-02
33	1.0200	1.0652	1.8618	82.2370	0.53057E-02
36	1.0209	1.0735	2.0455	87.7430	0.28196E-02

Table 14.

$a = 1,\ b = 2,\ c = 0.5,\ \rho_1 = 0.9,\ \rho_2 = 0,\ \delta = 0,\ \sigma_w^2 = 1,\ \sigma_z^2 = 10.$

STEPS	EG2	JOHA	VARL	VARD	S(h)
1	1.0080	0.9871	0.9851	8.1487	43.509
2	1.0146	0.9787	0.9799	15.8350	35.242
3	1.0204	0.9708	0.9760	22.9390	28.546
6	1.0425	0.9464	0.9627	40.6670	15.171
9	1.0374	0.9371	0.9697	58.2790	8.0623
12	1.0399	0.9097	0.9727	71.0830	4.2846
15	1.0332	0.9058	0.9934	80.8420	2.2770
18	1.0275	0.9052	1.0281	89.5440	1.2101
21	1.0289	0.8960	1.0727	99.5670	0.64310
24	1.0255	0.8919	1.1325	107.2500	0.34177
27	1.0410	0.9037	1.2151	114.4700	0.18163
30	1.0418	0.9061	1.3245	125.5500	0.96526E-01
33	1.0446	0.9170	1.4568	134.5300	0.51298E-01
36	1.0490	0.9350	1.6271	137.5800	0.27262E-01

Table 15.

$a = 1,\ b = 2,\ c = 0.5,\ \rho_1 = 0.9,\ \rho_2 = 0,\ \delta = 0.5,\ \sigma_w^2 = 1,\ \sigma_z^2 = 1.$

STEPS	EG2	JOHA	VARL	VARD	S(h)
1	1.0849	0.9972	1.0027	1.9379	4.5692
2	1.1423	0.9873	1.0127	3.9622	3.7011
3	1.1758	0.9894	1.0289	6.0131	2.9979
6	1.2347	0.9990	1.0958	11.9660	1.5932
9	1.2316	1.0138	1.1645	18.7340	0.84668
12	1.2249	1.0101	1.2069	25.6200	0.44996
15	1.2109	1.0159	1.2639	31.8580	0.23913
18	1.1955	1.0221	1.3264	37.9990	0.12708
21	1.1819	1.0311	1.4162	44.6290	0.67537E-01
24	1.1634	1.0379	1.5204	50.3610	0.35892E-01
27	1.1485	1.0468	1.6194	57.3480	0.19074E-01
30	1.1378	1.0533	1.7420	65.0460	0.10137E-01
33	1.1227	1.0716	1.8935	72.9960	0.53872E-02
36	1.1181	1.0774	2.0643	78.9510	0.28630E-02

Table 16.

$a = 1,\ b = 2,\ c = 0.5,\ \rho_1 = 0.9,\ \rho_2 = 0,\ \delta = 0.5,\ \sigma_w^2 = 1,\ \sigma_z^2 = 10.$

STEPS	EG2	JOHA	VARL	VARD	S(h)
1	1.0259	0.9560	0.9557	5.3721	44.756
2	1.0496	0.9304	0.9293	10.6040	36.252
3	1.0596	0.9160	0.9157	15.2390	29.365
6	1.0974	0.8787	0.8750	27.9820	15.606
9	1.1203	0.8606	0.8667	40.5310	8.2934
12	1.1499	0.8368	0.8685	49.7820	4.4075
15	1.1549	0.8336	0.8839	57.8210	2.3423
18	1.1643	0.8405	0.9227	65.7670	1.2448
21	1.1714	0.8302	0.9593	74.5770	0.66154
24	1.1703	0.8439	1.0249	81.1010	0.35157
27	1.1709	0.8582	1.0910	88.5840	0.18684
30	1.1717	0.8731	1.1881	97.6640	0.99293E-01
33	1.1654	0.9055	1.3035	105.0300	0.52768E-01
36	1.1724	0.9318	1.4227	109.7100	0.28043E-01

Table 17.

a = 0, b = 2, c = 0.5, ρ_1 = 0.5, ρ_2 = 0.05, δ = 0, σ_w^2 = 1, σ_z^2 = 1.

STEPS	EG2	JOHA	VARL	VARD
1	1.0545	1.0354	1.0549	1.0183
2	0.9300	0.9434	0.9754	0.9351
3	0.9345	0.9475	0.9948	0.9307
6	0.9486	0.9660	1.0933	0.9533
9	0.9625	0.9767	1.1582	0.9654
12	0.9767	0.9783	1.2137	0.9752
15	0.9795	0.9805	1.2800	0.9788
18	0.9842	0.9858	1.3614	0.9846
21	0.9853	0.9847	1.4352	0.9863
24	0.9852	0.9848	1.5090	0.9866
27	0.9875	0.9884	1.5868	0.9892
30	0.9861	0.9885	1.6658	0.9882
33	0.9865	0.9890	1.7706	0.9887
36	0.9909	0.9913	1.8840	0.9919

Table 18.

a = 0, b = 2, c = 0.5, ρ_1 = 0.5, ρ_2 = 0.05, δ = 0, σ_w^2 = 1, σ_z^2 = 10.

STEPS	EG2	JOHA	VARL	VARD
1	1.0858	0.9649	0.9814	0.9950
2	0.8719	0.8781	0.9102	0.9275
3	0.8876	0.8761	0.9269	0.9254
6	0.8942	0.9005	1.0253	0.9514
9	0.9181	0.9230	1.0940	0.9632
12	0.9403	0.9405	1.1667	0.9737
15	0.9484	0.9468	1.2399	0.9770
18	0.9599	0.9613	1.3349	0.9840
21	0.9617	0.9622	1.4091	0.9844
24	0.9613	0.9622	1.4799	0.9851
27	0.9706	0.9703	1.5531	0.9886
30	0.9716	0.9701	1.6164	0.9879
33	0.9730	0.9719	1.7225	0.9883
36	0.9760	0.9753	1.8240	0.9903

Table 19.

$a = 0,\ b = 2,\ c = 0.5,\ \rho_1 = 0.5,\ \rho_2 = 0.05,\ \delta = 0.5,\ \sigma_w^2 = 1,\ \sigma_z^2 = 1.$

STEPS	EG2	JOHA	VARL	VARD
1	1.2918	1.0283	1.0487	1.0168
2	1.1210	0.9319	0.9648	0.9286
3	1.1171	0.9331	0.9819	0.9229
6	1.0974	0.9558	1.0891	0.9480
9	1.0761	0.9693	1.1625	0.9620
12	1.0598	0.9741	1.2266	0.9722
15	1.0495	0.9764	1.2951	0.9770
18	1.0458	0.9825	1.3794	0.9826
21	1.0429	0.9825	1.4584	0.9849
24	1.0352	0.9825	1.5384	0.9854
27	1.0300	0.9852	1.6209	0.9879
30	1.0250	0.9856	1.7092	0.9870
33	1.0232	0.9859	1.8210	0.9875
36	1.0257	0.9879	1.9477	0.9909

Table 20.

$a = 0,\ b = 2,\ c = 0.5,\ \rho_1 = 0.5,\ \rho_2 = 0.05,\ \delta = 0.5,\ \sigma_w^2 = 1,\ \sigma_z^2 = 10.$

STEPS	EG2	JOHA	VARL	VARD
1	1.0159	0.9045	0.9182	0.9734
2	0.9425	0.8072	0.8378	0.9028
3	0.9285	0.8138	0.8653	0.9012
6	0.9685	0.8642	0.9787	0.9349
9	0.9792	0.9019	1.0660	0.9512
12	0.9892	0.9249	1.1518	0.9648
15	0.9905	0.9361	1.2254	0.9711
18	0.9946	0.9528	1.3170	0.9786
21	0.9946	0.9558	1.3859	0.9797
24	0.9945	0.9590	1.4543	0.9815
27	0.9963	0.9664	1.5215	0.9852
30	0.9968	0.9676	1.5894	0.9855
33	0.9970	0.9685	1.6878	0.9858
36	0.9982	0.9715	1.7912	0.9877

Table 21.

a = 0, b = 2, c = 0.5, ρ_1 = 0.9, ρ_2 = 0.05, δ = 0, σ_w^2 = 1, σ_z^2 = 1.

STEPS	EG2	JOHA	VARL	VARD
1	1.0862	1.0351	1.0479	1.0181
2	1.0157	0.9680	0.9910	0.9365
3	1.0112	0.9620	1.0014	0.9141
6	1.0185	0.9965	1.0874	0.9008
9	1.0223	1.0242	1.1580	0.8980
12	1.0277	1.0230	1.1920	0.9030
15	1.0143	1.0434	1.2616	0.9042
18	1.0085	1.0746	1.3427	0.9121
21	1.0146	1.0952	1.4237	0.9187
24	1.0053	1.1120	1.4934	0.9219
27	1.0033	1.1348	1.5682	0.9276
30	1.0023	1.1586	1.6486	0.9307
33	1.0022	1.1922	1.7459	0.9343
36	1.0077	1.2186	1.8530	0.9399

Table 22.

a = 0, b = 2, c = 0.5, ρ_1 = 0.9, ρ_2 = 0.05, δ = 0, σ_w^2 = 1, σ_z^2 = 10.

STEPS	EG2	JOHA	VARL	VARD
1	1.0932	1.0377	1.0440	1.0124
2	1.0289	0.9896	1.0016	0.9458
3	1.0208	0.9840	1.0035	0.9310
6	1.0340	1.0287	1.0823	0.9353
9	1.0218	1.0595	1.1428	0.9409
12	1.0166	1.0656	1.1799	0.9529
15	1.0002	1.0696	1.2301	0.9595
18	1.0057	1.1054	1.3136	0.9762
21	1.0140	1.1244	1.3936	0.9888
24	0.9976	1.1322	1.4483	0.9915
27	1.0028	1.1518	1.5173	0.9976
30	1.0084	1.1686	1.5747	1.0012
33	1.0100	1.1887	1.6589	1.0093
36	1.0184	1.2074	1.7515	1.0141

Table 23.

$a = 0,\ b = 2,\ c = 0.5,\ \rho_1 = 0.9,\ \rho_2 = 0.05,\ \delta = 0.5,\ \sigma_w^2 = 1,\ \sigma_z^2 = 1.$

STEPS	EG2	JOHA	VARL	VARD
1	1.0584	1.0353	1.0569	1.0180
2	0.9879	0.9557	0.9895	0.9303
3	0.9765	0.9442	0.9994	0.9039
6	0.9947	0.9581	1.0783	0.8813
9	0.9970	0.9700	1.1495	0.8728
12	1.0144	0.9679	1.1863	0.8737
15	1.0047	0.9860	1.2662	0.8717
18	1.0079	1.0094	1.3533	0.8770
21	1.0107	1.0315	1.4486	0.8827
24	1.0095	1.0501	1.5380	0.8863
27	1.0167	1.0662	1.6191	0.8920
30	1.0089	1.0905	1.7174	0.8960
33	1.0132	1.1177	1.8302	0.8999
36	1.0190	1.1410	1.9609	0.9060

Table 24.

$a = 0,\ b = 2,\ c = 0.5,\ \rho_1 = 0.9,\ \rho_2 = 0.05,\ \delta = 0.5,\ \sigma_w^2 = 1,\ \sigma_z^2 = 10.$

STEPS	EG2	JOHA	VARL	VARD
1	1.0634	1.0287	1.0366	1.0074
2	0.9935	0.9699	0.9842	0.9331
3	0.9785	0.9548	0.9798	0.9109
6	0.9827	0.9601	1.0231	0.8942
9	0.9666	0.9628	1.0562	0.8828
12	0.9684	0.9537	1.0818	0.8814
15	0.9538	0.9449	1.1160	0.8780
18	0.9573	0.9689	1.1875	0.8861
21	0.9626	0.9842	1.2604	0.8942
24	0.9572	0.9968	1.3142	0.8968
27	0.9573	1.0086	1.3749	0.9011
30	0.9567	1.0290	1.4368	0.9058
33	0.9622	1.0521	1.5175	0.9148
36	0.9657	1.0677	1.6031	0.9200

Table 25.

$a = 1,\ b = 2,\ c = 0.5,\ \rho_1 = 0.5,\ \rho_2 = 0.05,\ \delta = 0,\ \sigma_w^2 = 1,\ \sigma_z^2 = 1.$

STEPS	EG2	JOHA	VARL	VARD
1	1.0032	0.9632	0.9683	0.9983
2	1.0086	1.0206	1.0434	1.0638
3	1.0113	1.0254	1.0656	1.0715
6	1.0125	1.0175	1.1369	1.0511
9	1.0110	1.0156	1.2063	1.0371
12	1.0092	1.0069	1.2402	1.0294
15	1.0060	1.0054	1.3082	1.0239
18	1.0061	1.0065	1.3755	1.0209
21	1.0085	1.0072	1.4698	1.0183
24	1.0043	1.0022	1.5598	1.0147
27	1.0028	1.0021	1.6455	1.0124
30	1.0054	1.0061	1.7718	1.0128
33	1.0052	1.0059	1.9118	1.0121
36	1.0031	1.0015	2.0832	1.0086

Table 26.

$a = 1,\ b = 2,\ c = 0.5,\ \rho_1 = 0.5,\ \rho_2 = 0.05,\ \delta = 0,\ \sigma_w^2 = 1,\ \sigma_z^2 = 10.$

STEPS	EG2	JOHA	VARL	VARD
1	0.9942	0.8319	0.8325	0.9650
2	0.9485	0.8489	0.8568	1.0624
3	0.9755	0.8255	0.8443	1.0917
6	1.0007	0.8254	0.8810	1.0782
9	1.0048	0.8604	0.9654	1.0634
12	0.9989	0.8719	1.0275	1.0560
15	1.0057	0.8810	1.0954	1.0462
18	1.0127	0.9049	1.1874	1.0449
21	1.0200	0.9199	1.2935	1.0400
24	1.0113	0.9180	1.3702	1.0334
27	1.0192	0.9279	1.4682	1.0298
30	1.0213	0.9419	1.6167	1.0330
33	1.0239	0.9423	1.7494	1.0306
36	1.0147	0.9407	1.9032	1.0227

Table 27.

$a = 1,\ b = 2,\ c = 0.5,\ \rho_1 = 0.5,\ \rho_2 = 0.05,\ \delta = 0.5,\ \sigma_w^2 = 1,\ \sigma_z^2 = 1.$

STEPS	EG2	JOHA	VARL	VARD
1	1.1492	0.9229	0.9252	0.9752
2	1.1588	0.9557	0.9732	1.0250
3	1.1827	0.9724	1.0059	1.0317
6	1.1380	0.9943	1.1075	1.0241
9	1.1057	1.0020	1.1869	1.0191
12	1.0886	0.9992	1.2300	1.0160
15	1.0724	1.0008	1.2947	1.0136
18	1.0604	1.0003	1.3604	1.0120
21	1.0484	1.0022	1.4537	1.0102
24	1.0403	1.0013	1.5489	1.0076
27	1.0363	1.0003	1.6263	1.0064
30	1.0323	1.0036	1.7432	1.0067
33	1.0293	1.0050	1.8739	1.0069
36	1.0263	1.0011	2.0201	1.0044

Table 28.

$a = 1,\ b = 2,\ c = 0.5,\ \rho_1 = 0.5,\ \rho_2 = 0.05,\ \delta = 0.5,\ \sigma_w^2 = 1,\ \sigma_z^2 = 10.$

STEPS	EG2	JOHA	VARL	VARD
1	0.9128	0.7387	0.7394	0.9196
2	0.9074	0.7108	0.7132	1.0075
3	0.9262	0.6940	0.7054	1.0353
6	0.9539	0.7424	0.7846	1.0294
9	0.9721	0.7970	0.8899	1.0245
12	0.9884	0.8260	0.9785	1.0234
15	0.9897	0.8457	1.0623	1.0201
18	0.9959	0.8733	1.1662	1.0214
21	0.9969	0.8943	1.2731	1.0175
24	0.9924	0.9016	1.3723	1.0129
27	0.9963	0.9116	1.4812	1.0133
30	1.0035	0.9277	1.6435	1.0165
33	1.0015	0.9300	1.8002	1.0158
36	0.9958	0.9277	1.9778	1.0091

Table 29.

$a = 1,\ b = 2,\ c = 0.5,\ \rho_1 = 0.9,\ \rho_2 = 0.05,\ \delta = 0,\ \sigma_w^2 = 1,\ \sigma_z^2 = 1.$

STEPS	EG2	JOHA	VARL	VARD
1	1.0464	1.0231	1.0253	1.0054
2	1.1318	1.1054	1.1198	1.0698
3	1.1688	1.1463	1.1816	1.0944
6	1.2393	1.2219	1.3091	1.1239
9	1.2588	1.2704	1.4034	1.1365
12	1.2808	1.2605	1.4351	1.1412
15	1.2780	1.2846	1.5114	1.1468
18	1.2648	1.3028	1.5844	1.1416
21	1.2560	1.3180	1.6630	1.1339
24	1.2417	1.3260	1.7477	1.1300
27	1.2419	1.3449	1.8425	1.1259
30	1.2295	1.3572	1.9622	1.1211
33	1.2218	1.3965	2.1077	1.1164
36	1.2166	1.4217	2.2794	1.1114

Table 30.

$a = 1,\ b = 2,\ c = 0.5,\ \rho_1 = 0.9,\ \rho_2 = 0.05,\ \delta = 0,\ \sigma_w^2 = 1,\ \sigma_z^2 = 10.$

STEPS	EG2	JOHA	VARL	VARD
1	1.0315	0.9997	0.9986	0.9924
2	1.1465	1.1139	1.1129	1.0895
3	1.2082	1.1795	1.1794	1.1361
6	1.3357	1.2905	1.2916	1.2134
9	1.4088	1.3677	1.3788	1.2708
12	1.4932	1.3919	1.4286	1.3178
15	1.5321	1.4554	1.5101	1.3578
18	1.5478	1.5006	1.5798	1.3695
21	1.5524	1.5198	1.6402	1.3733
24	1.5566	1.5655	1.7275	1.3800
27	1.5888	1.6679	1.8621	1.3960
30	1.5763	1.7504	2.0271	1.3935
33	1.5794	1.8966	2.2608	1.3966
36	1.5887	2.1447	2.6062	1.3976

Table 31.

$a = 1,\ b = 2,\ c = 0.5,\ \rho_1 = 0.9,\ \rho_2 = 0.05,\ \delta = 0.5,\ \sigma_w^2 = 1,\ \sigma_z^2 = 1.$

STEPS	EG2	JOHA	VARL	VARD
1	1.1074	1.0125	1.0138	0.9995
2	1.1955	1.0625	1.0754	1.0404
3	1.2447	1.0863	1.1137	1.0525
6	1.3260	1.1406	1.2097	1.0573
9	1.3430	1.1789	1.2895	1.0554
12	1.3538	1.1685	1.3212	1.0499
15	1.3478	1.1810	1.3788	1.0481
18	1.3309	1.1981	1.4400	1.0400
21	1.3172	1.2110	1.5178	1.0328
24	1.2987	1.2292	1.6104	1.0298
27	1.2795	1.2514	1.7078	1.0265
30	1.2660	1.2746	1.8290	1.0246
33	1.2466	1.3214	1.9745	1.0222
36	1.2390	1.3467	2.1375	1.0202

Table 32.

$a = 1,\ b = 2,\ c = 0.5,\ \rho_1 = 0.9,\ \rho_2 = 0.05,\ \delta = 0.5,\ \sigma_w^2 = 1,\ \sigma_z^2 = 10.$

STEPS	EG2	JOHA	VARL	VARD
1	1.0340	0.9701	0.9702	0.9775
2	1.1522	1.0573	1.0545	1.0607
3	1.2164	1.1116	1.1054	1.1029
6	1.3555	1.1850	1.1661	1.1653
9	1.4524	1.2394	1.2190	1.2130
12	1.5516	1.2479	1.2423	1.2431
15	1.6038	1.2821	1.2850	1.2685
18	1.6303	1.3024	1.3174	1.2636
21	1.6406	1.2922	1.3337	1.2603
24	1.6622	1.3224	1.3925	1.2641
27	1.6684	1.3569	1.4497	1.2674
30	1.6592	1.3808	1.5341	1.2631
33	1.6576	1.4557	1.6616	1.2636
36	1.6727	1.5377	1.7990	1.2617

Chapter 11. Conclusions

The empirical evidence presented in this monograph is an attempt to revive the monetary model of exchange rate determination as a long run relationship. The interesting feature of this interpretation of the monetary model is that it allows for short run deviations of the exchange rate from its fundamentals.

In order to test this model we use data on three bilateral US$ exchange rates (British pound, German mark and Japanese yen) and other macroeconomic variables (money supply, industrial production, interest rate, and inflation), that traditionally enter the monetary approach to exchange rate determination.

Two econometric methodologies are used for testing this long run relationship. Engle and Granger's (1987) methodology, the most commonly used in empirical applications, turns out to be not very well design for the present case and the results that we obtain just point in this direction. The multivariate FIML estimation procedure of an ECM subject to cointegration developed by Johansen (1988b, 1991a), on the other hand, is appropriate.

Previous unfavorable empirical findings can be reinterpreted in the light of this theory. Cointegration between the exchange rate and its fundamentals is a necessary condition for the monetary model to hold in the long run. However, existence of cointegration is not a sufficient condition for its validity. Therefore, the empirical analysis proceeds in two steps: first, we test for the existence of cointegrating vectors and then, for their resemblance to a monetary equation of exchange rate determination.

The cointegrating vectors found using Johansen's methodology do not satisfy the restrictions that characterize the monetary equation. The rejection of those restrictions does not imply that the exchange rate is not related in a long run relationship with other variables in the system. We accept the hypothesis that the exchange rate enters at least in some of the cointegrating vectors.

The conclusion from these findings is that the original monetary model of exchange rate determination suffers from two types of misspecification. First, long run equilibrium relationship linking exchange rates and fundamentals are not unique. Secondly, those relationships do not reflect the typically assumed symmetry restrictions.

Tests for weak exogeneity of all the variables in the bilateral systems were carried out. The test is of particular interest when the variable being tested for exogeneity is the exchange rate. If the exchange rate is exogenous, the cointegrating residual does not enter the equation representing the short run dynamics of the exchange rate. Thus, the exchange rate is not driven by stationary deviations from those long run relations.

All the tests carried out in this monograph are likelihood ratio tests that rely on the assumption of normality of the disturbance term. In practice, the estimated residuals exhibit strong deviations from normality. Thus, we have considered it interesting to include a chapter where we analyze the empirical size and power of the likelihood ratio tests under deviations from normality. Likelihood ratio tests for cointegration are adversely affected by Cauchy disturbances in terms of their empirical size, and by ARCH disturbances in terms of their power. Cauchy disturbances downwards bias the size of the test for linear restrictions on the cointegrating vectors. Finally, the size of the test for restrictions on the loading matrix is jeopardize by Cauchy and, specially, ARCH disturbances.

We have found evidence that the exchange rate equation in the ECM does not include any past value of first differences of any of the elements of X_t. This evidence together with the fact that the exchange rate is weakly exogenous with respect to the cointegrating vectors is consistent with the observed random walk behavior of exchange rates.

We have analyzed predictive performance of the ECM. This is an implicit test for weak exogeneity since we are looking for an improvement in prediction when we include the error correction term in the ECM with respect to the case when the error correction term is omitted and, therefore, the ECM becomes a VAR in first differences. Thus the results of that prediction exercise also point towards the weak exogeneity of the exchange rate.

In recent years, modeling nonstationary time series has attracted the attention of econometricians, specially after the Nelson and Plosser (1982) study. The theory of cointegration allows testing economic theories linking nonstationary macroeconomic variables. However, little has been done in terms of evaluating the forecasting ability of cointegrated time series. Only the studies of Engle and Yoo (1987) and Ahn and Reinsel (1991) have analyzed prediction in cointegrated systems. These notes contribute to the study of prediction and further investigate the gain in forecasting accuracy from using those models.

We have studied the asymptotically efficient estimators of an ECM under all types of short and long run restrictions. The properties of the forecasts generated by this ECM were analyzed and the asymptotic mean squared error derived.

Chapter 9 deals with the prediction of three nominal dollar exchange rates. The aim is twofold. On the one hand, it is a further attempt to revive the old monetary model of exchange rate determination. On the other, it is an application of the theory of prediction with cointegrated time series. We have analyzed how restrictions on the short and long run parameters of the model can improve the forecasts of the three rates. In general, the imposition of restrictions helped predicting the rates. In fact, when the short run restrictions were imposed, there was an improvement in the short term forecast and when the long run constraints were imposed the long term forecast improved. However, a VAR in first differences, that assumes no cointegration, generates forecasts that are as good as the other models and in many cases better. An explanation for this outcome is that the exchange rate can be considered as weakly exogenous with respect to the cointegrating vectors. Even though there is cointegration between the exchange rate and some fundamentals, transitory deviations from the long run relationships do not affect the short run dynamics of the exchange rate. In this study we have only focused on the prediction of the exchange rate. However, the existence of cointegration implies that there is at least one variable in the system that will benefit, in terms of prediction, from the imposition of the cointegrating restrictions.

In a simulation exercise we compared the forecasting accuracy of an ECM estimated under different assumptions and also other models where the number of unit roots is misspecified. The results of the simulation show how, in some cases, when the system is close to being a fully nonstationary system, we could do better by not imposing the restrictions implied by the existence of cointegration. However, for not so extreme cases, the gain in predictive performance is important specially when compared with the underdifferenced model. When the Engle and Granger procedure was used, the gain in efficiency was much smaller compared to the Johansen's estimation procedure.

DATA APPENDIX

All the data series were obtained from DATA STREAM INTERNATIONAL, THE DUN & BRADSTREET CORPORATION. Below NGS stands for National Government Series and IMF for International Monetary Fund. The data was collected at the monthly frequency from January 1972 to March 1990. Two sample periods have been analyzed. In chapter 3 we use a sample period from January 1974 to December 1989. All the calculations in chapter 4 and 9, however, use the sample period, April 1973 to March 1986, leaving the observations from April 1986 to March 1990 for post sample prediction.

US data.

Consumer Price Index. Not seasonally adjusted, (all urban consumers). NGS.

Industrial production. Index, seasonally adjusted. NGS.

Money supply. Monetary survey, money (M1). Current prices. Not seasonally adjusted. $US mln. IMF.

Three month Treasury Bill Rate. End of period. NGS.

UK data.

Retail Price Index. All items. Not seasonally adjusted. NGS.

Output of the production industries. Index, seasonally adjusted. NGS.

Money Supply, M1. Current prices. Not seasonally adjusted. £UK mln. NGS (chapter 3) and IMF (chapter 4).

Three month Treasury Bill Rate. End of period. NGS.

Spot Exchange Rate UK£ to 1 US$. End of period. IMF.

Japan Data.

Consumer price index. National measure. Not seasonally adjusted. NGS.

Industrial production in mining and manufacturing. Seasonally adjusted. NGS.

Monetary survey. Money (M1) yen bln. Current prices. Not seasonally adjusted. IMF.

Call money rate. Money market rate 60B in IMF. Current prices. Not seasonally adjusted.

End of period exchange rate. ¥ to 1 US$. IMF.

West Germany Data.

Cost of living price index. Not seasonally adjusted. NGS.

Industrial production index. Seasonally adjusted. NGS.

Monetary survey. Money (M1). DM bln. IMF.

Call money rate. Money market rate 60B in IMF. Current prices. Not seasonally adjusted.

End of period exchange rate. DM to 1 US$. IMF.

BIBLIOGRAPHY

AHN, S. K. and G. C. REINSEL (1988), "Nested Reduced-Rank Autoregressive Models for Multiple Time Series." Journal of the American Statistical Association. vol.83, no. 403, pp. 849-856.

AHN, S. K. and G. C. REINSEL (1990), "Estimation for Partially Nonstationary Multivariate Autoregresive Models." Journal of the American Statistical Association. vol. 85, no. 411, pp. 813-823.

BAILLIE, R.T. and T. BOLLERSLEV (1989), "Common Stochastic Trends in a System of Exchange Rates." The Journal of Finance, vol XLIV, no 1, pp 167-181.

BAILLIE, R.T. and D.D. SELOVER (1987), "Cointegration and Models of Exchange Rate Determination." International Journal of Forecasting 3, pp. 43-51.

BAILLIE, R.T. and P. McMAHON (1990), "The Foreign Exchange Market: The Theory and Econometric Evidence." Cambridge University Press.

BANERJEE, A., J. J. DOLADO, D. F. HENDRY and G. W. SMITH, (1986), "Exploring Equilibrium Relationships in Econometrics Through Static Models: Some Monte Carlo Evidence." Oxford Bulletin of Economics and Statistics, vol. 48, pp. 253-277.

BILSON, J. F. O. (1978), "Rational Expectations and the Exchange Rate." in J. Frenkel and H. Jonhson eds. "The Economics of Exchange Rates." Addison-Wesley Press, Reading.

BOOTHE, P. and D. GLASSMAN (1987), "Off The Mark: Lessons For Exchange Rate Modeling." Oxford Economic Papers, pp. 443-457.

BOSSAERTS, P. (1988), "Common Nonstationary Components of

Asset Prices." Journal of Economic Dynamics and Control, vol 12, pp. 347-364.

CANOVA, F. (1990), "Are Exchange Rates Really Random Walks? Forecasting with a Bayesian Time Varying Coefficient Model." mimeo.

CHEUNG, Y.W. and K. S. LAI (1990), "Long-Run Purchasing Power Parity During The Recent Float." unpublished manuscript.

CHOW, G. R. (1990), "The Multiplier-Accelerator Model in The Light of Cointegration." mimeo.

CORBAE, D. and OULIARIS, S. (1988) "Cointegration and Tests of Purchasing Power Parity", Review of Economics and Statistics, 70 (3), pp 508-511.

CUMBY, R.E. and m. OBSTFELD (1984), "International Interest Rate and Price Level Linkages under Flexible Exchange Rates: A Review of Recent Evidence." in J.F.O. Bilson and R.C. Marston editors "Exchange Rate Theory and Practice." The University of Chicago Press for the NBER.

DAVIS, N. and P. NEWBOLD (1980), "Forecasting with Misspecified Models." Applied Statistics, vol 29, pp. 87-92.

DELGADO, F. and B. DUMAS (1990), "Monetary Contracting Between Central Banks and the Design of Sustainable Exchange Rate Zones. mimeo University of Pennsylvania.

DICKEY, D.A. and FULLER, W.A. (1979) "Distribution of The Estimators for Autoregressive Time Series with a Unit Root", JASA, Vol 74, No. 366.

DIEBOLD, F.X. (1986), "Rational Expectations, Random Walks and The Monetary Models of The Exchange Rate." Proceedings of the Business and Economics Statistics Section of the American Statistical Association, pp. 101-106.

DIEBOLD, F. X. and J. M. NASON (1990), "Nonparametric Exchange

Rate Prediction?" Journal of International economics.

DIEBOLD, F.X. and M. NERLOVE, (1990) "Unit Roots in Economic Time Series: A Selective Survey." in "Advances in Econometrics: Cointegration, Spurious Regression and Unit Roots." T.B.Fomby and G.F. Rhodes editors.

DIEBOLD, F.X. (1988) "Empirical Modeling Of Exchange Rate Dynamics." Lecture Notes in Economics and Mathematical Systems # 303, Springer-Verlag.

DORNBUSCH, R. (1976), "Expectations and Exchange Rate Dynamics", Journal of Political Economy 84, pp. 1161-1176.

ENDERS, W. (1988) "Arima and Cointegration of PPP Under Fixed and Flexible Exchange Rate Regimes", Review of Economics and Statistics, 70(3), pp 504-508.

ENDERS, W. (1989) "Unit Roots and the Real Exchange Rate before World War I: the Case of Britain and the USA" Journal of international and Finance, 8. pp 59 73.

ENGEL, C. and J.D. HAMILTON (1990), "Long Swings in the Dollar: Are they in the Data and Do Markets Know it?", The American Economic Review, vol 80, no 4, pp. 689-713.

ENGLE, R.F. (1987) "On The Theory of Cointegrated Economic Time Series, 1987." mimeo.

ENGLE, R.F. and C.W.J. GRANGER, (1987) "Co-Integration and Error Correction Representation, Estimation and Testing." Econometrica, vol. 55, No. 2, pp. 251-176.

ENGLE, R.F. D.F. HENDRY and J.F. RICHARD (1983), "Exogeneity." Econometrica, vol 51, pp. 277-304.

ENGLE, R.F. and B.S. YOO (1987), "Forecasting and Testing in Co-integrated Systems." Journal of Econometrics 35, pp. 143-159.

FINN, M. G. (1986), "Forecasting the Exchange Rate: A Monetary or a Random Walk Phenomenon?" Journal of International Money and Finance 5, pp. 181-193.

FRANKEL, J.A. (1979), "On The Mark: A Theory of Floating Exchange Rates Based on Real Interest Differentials." The American Economic Review 69, pp 611-622.

FRANKEL, J.A. (1984), "Test of Monetary and Portfolio Balance Models of Exchange Rate Determination." in J.F.O. Bilson and R.C. Marston editors "Exchange Rate Theory and Practice." The University of Chicago Press for the NBER.

FRENKEL, J.A. (1976), "A Monetary Approach to The Exchange Rate: Doctrinal Aspects and Empirical Evidence." Scandinavian Journal of Economics 78, 200-224.

FRENKEL, J.A. and M. L. MUSSA (1985), "Asset Markets, Exchange Rates and the Balance of Payments." Handbook of International Economics, R.W. Jones and P.B. Kenen editors, North-Holland.

FROOT, K.A. and M. OBSTFELD (1989a), "Exchange Rate Dynamics Under Stochastic Regime Shifts: A Unified Approach." NBER working paper no. 2835.

FROOT, K.A. and M. OBSTFELD (1989b), "Stochastic Process Switching: Some Simple Solutions" NBER working paper no. 2998.

FULLER, W.A. (1976), "Introduction to Statistical Time Series." New York, Wiley.

GARDEAZABAL, J. (1991), "The Monetary Model of Exchange Rate Determination in the Light of Cointegration." PhD Dissertation University of Pennsylvania.

GIAVAZZI, F. and A. GIOVANNINI (1989), "Limiting Exchange Rate Flexibility: The European Monetary System." The MIT Press.

GONZALO, J. (1989) "Comparison of Five Alternative Methods of Estimating Long Run Equilibrium Relationships." Discussion Paper 89-55, University of California, San Diego.

GRANGER, C. W. J. (1981), "Some Properties of Time Series Data and Their Use in Econometric Model Specification." Journal of Econometrics, vol. 16, pp. 121-130.

GRANGER, C. W. J. and P. NEWBOLD (1977), "Forecasting Economic Time Series", San Diego, Academic Press.

GUBITZ, A. (1988), "Collapse of the Purchasing Power Parity in the Light of Co-integrated Variables?", Weltwirtschaftliches Archiv, 124 (4), pp 667-674.

HAKKIO, C.S. and RUSH, M. (1989), "Market Efficiency and Cointegration: an Application to the Sterling and Dutschemark Exchange Markets", Journal of International Money and Finance, 8, pp. 75-88.

HALL, S.G. (1989) "Maximum Likelihood Estimation of Cointegration Vectors: An Example of The Johansen Procedure", Oxford Bulletin of Economics and Statistics, 51, 2.

HARVEY, A. C. (1989) "Forecasting, Structural Time Series Models and The Kalman Filter." Cambridge University Press.

HARVEY, A. C. and J. H. STOCK (1989), "Estimating Integrated Higher Order Continuous Time Autoregressions with an Application to Money-Income Causality." Journal of Econometrics, vol 42. pp. 319-336.

HENDRY, D.F. (1986) "Econometric Modeling with Cointegrated Variables: An Overview", Oxford Bulletin of Economics and Statistics, 48, 3.

HENDRY, D.F. and G.E. MIZON, (1989) "Evaluating Dynamic Econometric Models by Encompassing The VAR." mimeo, December.

HODRICK, R.J. (1987), "The Empirical Evidence on the

Efficiency of Forward and Futures Foreign Exchange Markets." Harwood Academic Publishers.

HOOPER, P. and J. E. MORTON (1982), "Fluctuations in the Dollar: A Model of Nominal and Real Exchange Rate Determination." Journal of International Money and Finance 1, pp. 39-56.

JOHANSEN, S. (1988a), "The Mathematical Structure of Error Correction Models." Contemporary Mathematics, vol 80, American Mathematical Society.

JOHANSEN, S. (1988b), "Statistical Analysis Of Cointegration Vectors", Journal of Economic Dynamics and Control, 12, pp 231-254. North-Holland.

JOHANSEN, S. and K. JUSELIUS (1990a) "Maximum Likelihood Estimation and Inference On Cointegration, With Applications To The Demand For Money." Oxford Bulletin Of Economics and Statistics, 52, 2, 169-210.

JOHANSEN, S. and K. JUSELIUS (1990b) "Some Structural Hypotheses in a Multivariate Cointegration Analysis of the Purchasing Power Parity and the Uncovered Interest Parity for UK." University of Copenhagen, preprint.

JOHANSEN, S. (1990c) "Cointegration in Partial Systems and the Efficiency of single equation analysis." University of Copenhagen, preprint.

JOHANSEN, S. (1991a) "Estimation and Hypothesis Testing of Cointegration Vectors in Gaussian Vector Autoregressive Models.", Econometrica.

JOHANSEN, S. (1991b) "Determination of Cointegration Rank in The Presence of a Linear Trend." Department of Statistics University of Helsinki Research Report # 76.

KLEIN, M.W. (1989), "Playing With The Band: Dynamic Effects of Target Zones in an Open Economy." mimeo, Clark University.

KRUGMAN, P.R. (1988), "Target Zones and Exchange Rate Dynamics", NBER working paper no. 2481.

LEE, H.S. (1989), "Maximum Likelihood Inferences on Cointegration and Seasonal Cointegration." University of California, San Diego. Discussion Paper 89-19.

LEVICH, R. M. (1985), "Empirical Studies of Exchange Rates: Price Behavior, Rate Determination and Market Efficiency." in The Handbook of Internatinal Economics vol 2, R. W. Jones and P. B. Kenen editors, North Holland.

LUCEY, B.M. (1988), "Efficiency in the Forward Exchange Market: An Application of Cointegration", The Economic and Social Review, Vol. 20, No. 1, pp 25-36.

LÜTKEPOHL, H. and H. E. REIMERS (1990), "Impulse Response Analysis of Co-Integrated Systems with an Application to German Money Demand." mimeo, Institut für Statistik und Ökonometrie der Christian-Albrechts-Universität Kiel.

MacDONALD, R.and TAYLOR, M.P. (1989), "Foreign Exchange Market Efficiency and Cointegration: Some Evidence from the Recent Float", Economics Letters, 29, pp. 63-68.

MARK, C. (1990), "Real and Nominal Rates in the Long Run: An Empirical Investigation." Journal of International Economics, 28, pp 115-136.

MEESE, R.A. and K. ROGOFF (1983), "Empirical Exchange Rate Models Of The Seventies, Do They Fit Out Of Sample?" Journal of International Economics, 14, pp. 3-24.

MEESE, R.A. and K.J. SINGLETON (1982), "A Note on Unit Roots and the Empirical Modeling of Exchange Rates." Journal of Finance 37, pp. 1029-36.

MILLER, M. and P. WELLER (1988), "The Stabilizing Properties of Target Zones" mimeo University of Warwick.

MIZRACH, B. (1990), "Multivariate Nearest Neighbor Forecasts of EMS Exchange Rates", mimeo.

MUSSA, M. (1984), "The Theory of Exchange Rate Determination." in J.F.O. Bilson and R.C. Marston editors "Exchange Rate Theory and Practice." The University of Chicago Press for the NBER.

MUSSA, M. (1983), "Empirical Regularities in The Behavior of Exchange Rates and Theories of The Foreign Exchange Market." in Theory, Policy, Institutions: Papers from the Carnegie-Rochester Conference Series on Public Policy, Karl Brunner and Alan Meltzer eds. North-Holland.

NELSON, C.R. and C.I. PLOSSER (1982), "Trends and Random Walks in Macroeconomic Time Series, some Evidence and Implications." Journal of Monetary Economics, 10, pp. 139-162.

NERLOVE, M., D. M. GRETHER and J. L. CARVALHO (1979), "Analysis of Economic Time Series: A Synthesis." Academic Press.

REGULEZ, M. (1991), "Prediction in Cointegrated Systems: Theory and Applications." PhD Dissertation, University of Pennsylvania.

REINSEL, G. and S. K. AHN (1991), "Vector AR Models with Unit Roots and Reduced Rank Structure: Estimation, Likelihood Ratio Test and Forecasting." to appear in The Journal of Time Series Analysis.

OBSTFELD, M. (1988), "The effectiveness of Foreign-Exchange Intervention: Recent Experience." University of Pennsylvania Disscusion Paper.

OSTERWALD-LENUM, M. (1990), "Recalculated and Extended Tables of the Asymptotic Distribution of Some Important Maximum Likelihood Cointegration Test Statistics" Institute of Economics, University of Copenhagen.

PHILLIPS, P.C.B. (1986), "Understanding Spurious Regressions in Econometrics." Journal of Econometrics, 33, pp. 311-340.

PHILLIPS, P.C.B. (1987), "Time series regression with a unit root." Econometrica 55, pp. 277-301.

PHILLIPS, P.C.B. (1989), "Optimal Inference in Cointegrated Systems" Cowless Foundation Discussion Paper # 866.

PHILLIPS, P.C.B. (1989), "Error Correction and Long Run Equilibria in Continuous Time." Cowless Foundation Discussion Paper # 882R.

PHILLIPS, P.C.B. and P. PERRON (1988), "Testing for unit root in time series regression" Biometrica, Vol. 75, No. 2, pp 335-46.

PHILLIPS, P.C.B. and S. N. DURLAUF (1986), "Multiple Time Series Regression with Integrated Processes." Review of Economic Studies, vol LIII, pp. 473-95.

PHILLIPS, P.C.B. and OULIARIS, S. (1990), "Asymptotic Properties of Residual Based Tests for Cointegration", Econometrica, Vol.58, No. 1 pp. 165-193.

SCHINASI, G. J. and P.A.V.B. SWAMY, (1989), "The Out-of-Sample Forecasting Performance of Exchange Rate Models When Coefficients are Allowed to Change." Journal of International Money and Finance 8, pp. 375-390.

SCHMIDT, P. (1974), "The Asymptotic Distribution of Forecasts in the Dynamic Simulation of an Econometric Model." Econometrica, vol. 42, pp. 303-309.

SIMS, C.A., J.H. STOCK and M.W. WATSON (1990), "Inference in

Linear Time Series Models with some Unit Roots." Econometrica.

SOMANATH, V. S. (1986), "Efficient Exchange Rate Forecasts: Lagged Models Better than Random Walks." Journal of International Money and Finance 5, pp. 195-220.

STARCK, C. (1990), "Foreign and Domestic Shocks and Fluctuations in the Finnish Economy 1960-1988. Bank of Findland Publications, Series B:44.

STOCK, J. H. (1987), "Asymptotic Properties of Least Squares Estimators of Cointegrating Vectors." Econometrica, vol. 55, pp. 1035-1056.

STOCK, J. H. and M. W. WATSON, (1988), "Testing For Common Trends." Journal of The American Statistical Association. vol 83, no. 404, pp. 1097-1107.

SVENSSON, L.E.O. (1989), "Target Zones and Interest Rate Variability." mimeo.

THOM, R. (1989), "Real Exchange Rates, Cointegration and Purchasing Power Parity: Irish Experience in the EMS", The Economic and Social Review, Vol. 20, No. 2, pp. 147-163.

VELU, R. P., G. C. REINSEL and D. W. WICHERN (1986), "Reduced Rank Models for Multiple Time Series." Biometrika 73, 1, pp. 105-118.

WOLFF, C. C. P. (1988), "Exchange Rates, Innovations and Forecasting", Journal of International Money and Finance 7, pp. 49-61.

WOO, W.T. (1985), "The Monetary Approach to Exchange Rate Determination under Rational Expectations." Journal of International Economics, 18, pp. 1-16.

Lecture Notes in Economics and Mathematical Systems

For information about Vols. 1–210
please contact your bookseller or Springer-Verlag

Vol. 211: P. van den Heuvel, The Stability of a Macroeconomic System with Quantity Constraints. VII, 169 pages. 1983.

Vol. 212: R. Sato and T. Nôno, Invariance Principles and the Structure of Technology. V, 94 pages. 1983.

Vol. 213: Aspiration Levels in Bargaining and Economic Decision Making. Proceedings, 1982. Edited by R. Tietz. VIII, 406 pages. 1983.

Vol. 214: M. Faber, H. Niemes und G. Stephan, Entropie, Umweltschutz und Rohstoffverbrauch. IX, 181 Seiten. 1983.

Vol. 215: Semi-Infinite Programming and Applications. Proceedings, 1981. Edited by A.V. Fiacco and K.O. Kortanek. XI, 322 pages. 1983.

Vol. 216: H.H. Müller, Fiscal Policies in a General Equilibrium Model with Persistent Unemployment. VI, 92 pages. 1983.

Vol. 217: Ch. Grootaert, The Relation Between Final Demand and Income Distribution. XIV, 105 pages. 1983.

Vol 218: P. van Loon, A Dynamic Theory of the Firm: Production, Finance and Investment. VII, 191 pages. 1983.

Vol. 219: E. van Damme, Refinements of the Nash Equilibrium Concept. VI. 151 pages. 1983.

Vol. 220: M. Aoki, Notes on Economic Time Series Analysis: System Theoretic Perspectives. IX, 249 pages. 1983.

Vol. 221: S. Nakamura, An Inter-Industry Translog Model of Prices and Technical Change for the West German Economy. XIV, 290 pages. 1984.

Vol. 222: P. Meier, Energy Systems Analysis for Developing Countries. VI, 344 pages. 1984.

Vol. 223: W. Trockel, Market Demand. VIII, 205 pages. 1984.

Vol. 224: M. Kiy, Ein disaggregiertes Prognosesystem fur die Bundesrepublik Deutschland. XVIII, 276 Seiten. 1984.

Vol. 225: T.R. von Ungern-Sternberg, Zur Analyse von Märkten mit unvollständiger Nachfragerinformaton. IX, 125 Seiten. 1984.

Vol. 226: Selected Topics in Operations Research and Mathematical Economics. Proceedings, 1963. Edited by G. Hammer and D. Pallaschke IX, 478 pages. 1984.

Vol. 227: Risk and Capital. Proceedings, 1983. Edited by G. Bamberg and K. Spremann VII, 306 pages. 1984.

Vol. 228: Nonlinear Models of Fluctuating Growth. Proceedings, 1983. Edited by R.M. Goodwin, M. Krüger and A. Vercelli. XVII, 277 pages. 1984.

Vol. 229: Interactive Decision Analysis. Proceedings, 1983. Edited by M. Grauer and A.P. Wierzbicki. VIII, 269 pages. 1984.

Vol. 230: Macro-Economic Planning with Conflicting Goals. Proceedings, 1982. Edited by M. Despontin, P. Nijkamp and J. Spronk. VI, 297 pages. 1984.

Vol. 231: G.F. Newell, The M/M/8 Service System with Ranked Servers in Heavy Traffic. XI, 126 pages. 1984.

Vol. 232: L. Bauwens, Bayesian Full Information Analysis of Simultaneous Equation Models Using Integration by Monte Carlo. VI, 114 pages. 1984.

Vol. 233: G. Wagenhals, The World Copper Market. XI, 190 pages. 1984.

Vol. 234: B.C. Eaves, A Course in Triangulations for Solving Equations with Deformations. III, 302 pages. 1984.

Vol. 235: Stochastic Models in Reliability Theory Proceedings, 1984. Edited by S. Osaki and Y. Hatoyama. VII, 212 pages. 1984.

Vol. 236: G. Gandolfo, P.C. Padoan, A Disequilibrium Model of Real and Financial Accumulation in an Open Economy. VI, 172 pages. 1984.

Vol. 237: Misspecification Analysis. Proceedings, 1983. Edited by T.K. Dijkstra. V, 129 pages. 1984.

Vol. 238: W. Domschke, A. Drexl, Location and Layout Planning. IV, 134 pages. 1985.

Vol. 239: Microeconomic Models of Housing Markets. Edited by K. Stahl. VII, 197 pages. 1985.

Vol. 240: Contributions to Operations Research. Proceedings, 1984. Edited by K. Neumann and D. Pallaschke. V, 190 pages. 1985.

Vol. 241: U. Wittmann, Das Konzept rationaler Preiserwartungen. XI, 310 Seiten. 1985.

Vol. 242: Decision Making with Multiple Objectives. Proceedings, 1984. Edited by Y.Y. Haimes and V. Chankong. XI, 571 pages. 1985.

Vol. 243: Integer Programming and Related Areas. A Classified Bibliography 1981–1984. Edited by R. von Randow. XX, 386 pages. 1985.

Vol. 244: Advances in Equilibrium Theory. Proceedings, 1984. Edited by C.D. Aliprantis, O. Burkinshaw and N.J. Rothman. II, 235 pages. 1985.

Vol. 245: J.E.M. Wilhelm, Arbitrage Theory. VII, 114 pages. 1985.

Vol. 246: P.W. Otter, Dynamic Feature Space Modelling, Filtering and Self-Tuning Control of Stochastic Systems. XIV, 177 pages.1985.

Vol. 247: Optimization and Discrete Choice in Urban Systems. Proceedings, 1983. Edited by B.G. Hutchinson, P. Nijkamp and M. Batty VI, 371 pages. 1985.

Vol. 248: Pural Rationality and Interactive Decision Processes. Proceedings, 1984. Edited by M. Grauer, M. Thompson and A.P. Wierzbicki. VI, 354 pages. 1985.

Vol. 249: Spatial Price Equilibrium: Advances in Theory, Computation and Application. Proceedings, 1984. Edited by P.T. Harker. VII, 277 pages. 1985.

Vol. 250: M. Roubens, Ph. Vincke, Preference Modelling. VIII, 94 pages. 1985.

Vol. 251: Input-Output Modeling. Proceedings, 1984. Edited by A. Smyshlyaev. VI, 261 pages. 1985.

Vol. 252: A. Birolini, On the Use of Stochastic Processes in Modeling Reliability Problems. VI, 105 pages. 1985.

Vol. 253: C. Withagen, Economic Theory and International Trade in Natural Exhaustible Resources. VI, 172 pages. 1985.

Vol. 254: S. Müller, Arbitrage Pricing of Contingent Claims. VIII, 151 pages. 1985.

Vol. 255: Nondifferentiable Optimization: Motivations and Applications. Proceedings, 1984. Edited by V.F. Demyanov and D. Pallaschke. VI, 350 pages. 1985.

Vol. 256: Convexity and Duality in Optimization. Proceedings, 1984. Edited by J. Ponstein. V, 142 pages. 1985.

Vol. 257: Dynamics of Macrosystems. Proceedings, 1984. Edited by J.-P. Aubin, D. Saari and K. Sigmund. VI, 280 pages. 1985.

Vol. 258: H. Funke, Eine allgemeine Theorie der Polypol- und Oligopolpreisbildung. III, 237 pages. 1985.

Vol. 259: Infinite Programming. Proceedings, 1984. Edited by E.J. Anderson and A.B. Philpott. XIV, 244 pages. 1985.

Vol. 260: H.-J. Kruse, Degeneracy Graphs and the Neighbourhood Problem. VIII, 128 pages. 1986.

Vol. 261: Th.R. Gulledge, Jr., N.K. Womer, The Economics of Made-to-Order Production. VI, 134 pages. 1986.

Vol. 262: H.U. Buhl, A Neo-Classical Theory of Distribution and Wealth. V, 146 pages. 1986.

Vol. 263: M. Schäfer, Resource Extraction and Market Struucture. XI, 154 pages. 1986.

Vol. 264: Models of Economic Dynamics. Proceedings, 1983. Edited by H.F. Sonnenschein. VII, 212 pages. 1986.

Vol. 265: Dynamic Games and Applications in Economics. Edited by T. Basar. IX, 288 pages. 1986.

Vol. 266: Multi-Stage Production Planning and Inventory Control. Edited by S. Axsäter, Ch. Schneeweiss and E. Silver. V, 264 pages.1986.

Vol. 267: R. Bemelmans, The Capacity Aspect of Inventories. IX, 165 pages. 1986.

Vol. 268: V. Firchau, Information Evaluation in Capital Markets. VII, 103 pages. 1986.

Vol. 269: A. Borglin, H. Keiding, Optimality in Infinite Horizon Economies. VI, 180 pages. 1986.

Vol. 270: Technological Change, Employment and Spatial Dynamics. Proceedings, 1985. Edited by P. Nijkamp. VII, 466 pages. 1986.

Vol. 271: C. Hildreth, The Cowles Commission in Chicago, 1939–1955. V, 176 pages. 1986.

Vol. 272: G. Clemenz, Credit Markets with Asymmetric Information. VIII,212 pages. 1986.

Vol. 273: Large-Scale Modelling and Interactive Decision Analysis. Proceedings, 1985. Edited by G. Fandel, M. Grauer, A. Kurzhanski and A.P. Wierzbicki. VII, 363 pages. 1986.

Vol. 274: W.K. Klein Haneveld, Duality in Stochastic Linear and Dynamic Programming. VII, 295 pages. 1986.

Vol. 275: Competition, Instability, and Nonlinear Cycles. Proceedings, 1985. Edited by W. Semmler. XII, 340 pages. 1986.

Vol. 276: M.R. Baye, D.A. Black, Consumer Behavior, Cost of Living Measures, and the Income Tax. VII, 119 pages. 1986.

Vol. 277: Studies in Austrian Capital Theory, Investment and Time. Edited by M. Faber. VI, 317 pages. 1986.

Vol. 278: W.E. Diewert, The Measurement of the Economic Benefits of Infrastructure Services. V, 202 pages. 1986.

Vol. 279: H.-J. Büttler, G. Frei and B. Schips, Estimation of Disequilibrium Modes. VI, 114 pages. 1986.

Vol. 280: H.T. Lau, Combinatorial Heuristic Algorithms with FORTRAN. VII, 126 pages. 1986.

Vol. 281: Ch.-L. Hwang, M.-J. Lin, Group Decision Making under Multiple Criteria. XI, 400 pages. 1987.

Vol. 282: K. Schittkowski, More Test Examples for Nonlinear Programming Codes. V, 261 pages. 1987.

Vol. 283: G. Gabisch, H.-W. Lorenz, Business Cycle Theory. VII, 229 pages. 1987.

Vol. 284: H. Lütkepohl, Forecasting Aggregated Vector ARMA Processes. X, 323 pages. 1987.

Vol. 285: Toward Interactive and Intelligent Decision Support Systems. Volume 1. Proceedings, 1986. Edited by Y. Sawaragi, K. Inoue and H. Nakayama. XII, 445 pages. 1987.

Vol. 286: Toward Interactive and Intelligent Decision Support Systems. Volume 2. Proceedings, 1986. Edited by Y. Sawaragi, K. Inoue and H. Nakayama. XII, 450 pages. 1987.

Vol. 287: Dynamical Systems. Proceedings, 1985. Edited by A.B. Kurzhanski and K. Sigmund. VI, 215 pages. 1987.

Vol. 288: G.D. Rudebusch, The Estimation of Macroeconomic Disequilibrium Models with Regime Classification Information. VII,128 pages. 1987.

Vol. 289: B.R. Meijboom, Planning in Decentralized Firms. X, 168 pages. 1987.

Vol. 290: D.A. Carlson, A. Haurie, Infinite Horizon Optimal Control. XI, 254 pages. 1987.

Vol. 291: N. Takahashi, Design of Adaptive Organizations. VI, 140 pages. 1987.

Vol. 292: I. Tchijov, L. Tomaszewicz (Eds.), Input-Output Modeling. Proceedings, 1985. VI, 195 pages. 1987.

Vol. 293: D. Batten, J. Casti, B. Johansson (Eds.), Economic Evolution and Structural Adjustment. Proceedings, 1985. VI, 382 pages.

Vol. 294: J. Jahn, W. Knabs (Eds.), Recent Advances and Historical Development of Vector Optimization. VII, 405 pages. 1987.

Vol. 295. H. Meister, The Purification Problem for Constrained Games with Incomplete Information. X, 127 pages. 1987.

Vol. 296: A. Börsch-Supan, Econometric Analysis of Discrete Choice. VIII, 211 pages. 1987.

Vol. 297: V. Fedorov, H. Läuter (Eds.), Model-Oriented Data Analysis. Proceedings, 1987. VI, 239 pages. 1988.

Vol. 298: S.H. Chew, Q. Zheng, Integral Global Optimization. VII, 179 pages. 1988.

Vol. 299: K. Marti, Descent Directions and Efficient Solutions in Discretely Distributed Stochastic Programs. XIV, 178 pages. 1988.

Vol. 300: U. Derigs, Programming in Networks and Graphs. XI, 315 pages. 1988.

Vol. 301: J. Kacprzyk, M. Roubens (Eds.), Non-Conventional Preference Relations in Decision Making. VII, 155 pages. 1988.

Vol. 302: H.A. Eiselt, G. Pederzoli (Eds.), Advances in Optimization and Control. Proceedings, 1986. VIII, 372 pages. 1988.

Vol. 303: F.X. Diebold, Empirical Modeling of Exchange Rate Dynamics. VII, 143 pages. 1988.

Vol. 304: A. Kurzhanski, K. Neumann, D. Pallaschke (Eds.), Optimization, Parallel Processing and Applications. Proceedings, 1987. VI, 292 pages. 1988.

Vol. 305: G.-J.C.Th. van Schijndel, Dynamic Firm and Investor Behaviour under Progressive Personal Taxation. X, 215 pages.1988.

Vol. 306: Ch. Klein, A Static Microeconomic Model of Pure Competition. VIII, 139 pages. 1988.

Vol. 307: T.K. Dijkstra (Ed.), On Model Uncertainty and its Statistical Implications. VII, 138 pages. 1988.

Vol. 308: J.R. Daduna, A. Wren (Eds.), Computer-Aided Transit Scheduling. VIII, 339 pages. 1988.

Vol. 309: G. Ricci, K. Velupillai (Eds.), Growth Cycles and Multisectoral Economics: the Goodwin Tradition. III, 126 pages. 1988.

Vol. 310: J. Kacprzyk, M. Fedrizzi (Eds.), Combining Fuzzy Imprecision with Probabilistic Uncertainty in Decision Making. IX, 399 pages. 1988.

Vol. 311: R. Färe, Fundamentals of Production Theory. IX, 163 pages. 1988.

Vol. 312: J. Krishnakumar, Estimation of Simultaneous Equation Models with Error Components Structure. X, 357 pages. 1988.

Vol. 313: W. Jammernegg, Sequential Binary Investment Decisions. VI, 156 pages. 1988.

Vol. 314: R. Tietz, W. Albers, R. Selten (Eds.), Bounded Rational Behavior in Experimental Games and Markets. VI, 368 pages. 1988.

Vol. 315: I. Orishimo, G.J.D. Hewings, P. Nijkamp (Eds), Information Technology: Social and Spatial Perspectives. Proceedings 1986. VI, 268 pages. 1988.

Vol. 316: R.L. Basmann, D.J. Slottje, K. Hayes, J.D. Johnson, D.J. Molina, The Generalized Fechner-Thurstone Direct Utility Function and Some of its Uses. VIII, 159 pages. 1988.

Vol. 317: L. Bianco, A. La Bella (Eds.), Freight Transport Planning and Logistics. Proceedings, 1987. X, 568 pages. 1988.

Vol. 318: T. Doup, Simplicial Algorithms on the Simplotope. VIII, 262 pages. 1988.

Vol. 319: D.T. Luc, Theory of Vector Optimization. VIII, 173 pages. 1989.

Vol. 320: D. van der Wijst, Financial Structure in Small Business. VII, 181 pages. 1989.

Vol. 321: M. Di Matteo, R.M. Goodwin, A. Vercelli (Eds.), Technological and Social Factors in Long Term Fluctuations. Proceedings. IX, 442 pages. 1989.

Vol. 322: T. Kollintzas (Ed.), The Rational Expectations Equilibrium Inventory Model. XI, 269 pages. 1989.

Vol. 323: M.B.M. de Koster, Capacity Oriented Analysis and Design of Production Systems. XII, 245 pages. 1989.

Vol. 324: I.M. Bomze, B.M. Pötscher, Game Theoretical Foundations of Evolutionary Stability. VI, 145 pages. 1989.

Vol. 325: P. Ferri, E. Greenberg, The Labor Market and Business Cycle Theories. X, 183 pages. 1989.

Vol. 326: Ch. Sauer, Alternative Theories of Output, Unemployment, and Inflation in Germany: 1960–1985. XIII, 206 pages. 1989.

Vol. 327: M. Tawada, Production Structure and International Trade. V, 132 pages. 1989.

Vol. 328: W. Güth, B. Kalkofen, Unique Solutions for Strategic Games. VII, 200 pages. 1989.

Vol. 329: G. Tillmann, Equity, Incentives, and Taxation. VI, 132 pages. 1989.

Vol. 330: P.M. Kort, Optimal Dynamic Investment Policies of a Value Maximizing Firm. VII, 185 pages. 1989.

Vol. 331: A. Lewandowski, A.P. Wierzbicki (Eds.), Aspiration Based Decision Support Systems. X, 400 pages. 1989.

Vol. 332: T.R. Gulledge, Jr., L.A. Litteral (Eds.), Cost Analysis Applications of Economics and Operations Research. Proceedings. VII, 422 pages. 1989.

Vol. 333: N. Dellaert, Production to Order. VII, 158 pages. 1989.

Vol. 334: H.-W. Lorenz, Nonlinear Dynamical Economics and Chaotic Motion. XI, 248 pages. 1989.

Vol. 335: A.G. Lockett, G. Islei (Eds.), Improving Decision Making in Organisations. Proceedings. IX, 606 pages. 1989.

Vol. 336: T. Puu, Nonlinear Economic Dynamics. VII, 119 pages. 1989.

Vol. 337: A. Lewandowski, I. Stanchev (Eds.), Methodology and Software for Interactive Decision Support. VIII, 309 pages. 1989.

Vol. 338: J.K. Ho, R.P. Sundarraj, DECOMP: an Implementation of Dantzig-Wolfe Decomposition for Linear Programming. VI, 206 pages.

Vol. 339: J. Terceiro Lomba, Estimation of Dynamic Econometric Models with Errors in Variables. VIII, 116 pages. 1990.

Vol. 340: T. Vasko, R. Ayres, L. Fontvieille (Eds.), Life Cycles and Long Waves. XIV, 293 pages. 1990.

Vol. 341: G.R. Uhlich, Descriptive Theories of Bargaining. IX, 165 pages. 1990.

Vol. 342: K. Okuguchi, F. Szidarovszky, The Theory of Oligopoly with Multi-Product Firms. V, 167 pages. 1990.

Vol. 343: C. Chiarella, The Elements of a Nonlinear Theory of Economic Dynamics. IX, 149 pages. 1990.

Vol. 344: K. Neumann, Stochastic Project Networks. XI, 237 pages. 1990.

Vol. 345: A. Cambini, E. Castagnoli, L. Martein, P Mazzoleni, S. Schaible (Eds.), Generalized Convexity and Fractional Programming with Economic Applications. Proceedings, 1988. VII, 361 pages. 1990.

Vol. 346: R. von Randow (Ed.), Integer Programming and Related Areas. A Classified Bibliography 1984–1987. XIII, 514 pages. 1990.

Vol. 347: D. Ríos Insua, Sensitivity Analysis in Multi-objective Decision Making. XI, 193 pages. 1990.

Vol. 348: H. Störmer, Binary Functions and their Applications. VIII, 151 pages. 1990.

Vol. 349: G.A. Pfann, Dynamic Modelling of Stochastic Demand for Manufacturing Employment. VI, 158 pages. 1990.

Vol. 350: W.-B. Zhang, Economic Dynamics. X, 232 pages. 1990.

Vol. 351: A. Lewandowski, V. Volkovich (Eds.), Multiobjective Problems of Mathematical Programming. Proceedings, 1988. VII, 315 pages. 1991.

Vol. 352: O. van Hilten, Optimal Firm Behaviour in the Context of Technological Progress and a Business Cycle. XII, 229 pages. 1991.

Vol. 353: G. Ricci (Ed.), Decision Processes in Economics. Proceedings, 1989. III, 209 pages 1991.

Vol. 354: M. Ivaldi, A Structural Analysis of Expectation Formation. XII, 230 pages. 1991.

Vol. 355: M. Salomon. Deterministic Lotsizing Models for Production Planning. VII, 158 pages. 1991.

Vol. 356: P. Korhonen, A. Lewandowski, J . Wallenius (Eds.), Multiple Criteria Decision Support. Proceedings, 1989. XII, 393 pages. 1991.

Vol. 357: P. Zörnig, Degeneracy Graphs and Simplex Cycling. XV, 194 pages. 1991.

Vol. 358: P. Knottnerus, Linear Models with Correlated Disturbances. VIII, 196 pages. 1991.

Vol. 359: E. de Jong, Exchange Rate Determination and Optimal Economic Policy Under Various Exchange Rate Regimes. VII, 270 pages. 1991.

Vol. 360: P. Stalder, Regime Translations, Spillovers and Buffer Stocks. VI, 193 pages . 1991.

Vol. 361: C. F. Daganzo, Logistics Systems Analysis. X, 321 pages. 1991.

Vol. 362: F. Gehrels, Essays In Macroeconomics of an Open Economy. VII, 183 pages. 1991.

Vol. 363: C. Puppe, Distorted Probabilities and Choice under Risk. VIII, 100 pages . 1991

Vol. 364: B. Horvath, Are Policy Variables Exogenous? XII, 162 pages. 1991.

Vol. 365: G. A. Heuer, U. Leopold-Wildburger. Balanced Silverman Games on General Discrete Sets. V, 140 pages. 1991.

Vol. 366: J. Gruber (Ed.), Econometric Decision Models. Proceedings, 1989. VIII, 636 pages. 1991.

Vol. 367: M. Grauer, D. B. Pressmar (Eds.), Parallel Computing and Mathematical Optimization. Proceedings. V, 208 pages. 1991.

Vol. 368: M. Fedrizzi, J. Kacprzyk, M. Roubens (Eds.), Interactive Fuzzy Optimization. VII, 216 pages. 1991.

Vol. 369: R. Koblo, The Visible Hand. VIII, 131 pages.1991.

Vol. 370: M. J. Beckmann, M. N. Gopalan, R. Subramanian (Eds.), Stochastic Processes and their Applications. Proceedings, 1990. XLI, 292 pages. 1991.

Vol. 371: A. Schmutzler, Flexibility and Adjustment to Information in Sequential Decision Problems. VIII, 198 pages. 1991.

Vol. 372: J. Esteban, The Social Viability of Money. X, 202 pages. 1991.

Vol. 373: A. Billot, Economic Theory of Fuzzy Equilibria. XIII, 164 pages. 1992.

Vol. 374: G. Pflug, U. Dieter (Eds.), Simulation and Optimization. Proceedings, 1990. X, 162 pages. 1992.

Vol. 375: S.-J. Chen, Ch.-L. Hwang, Fuzzy Multiple Attribute Decision Making. XII, 536 pages. 1992.

Vol. 376: K.-H. Jöckel, G. Rothe, W. Sendler (Eds.), Bootstrapping and Related Techniques. Proceedings, 1990. VIII, 247 pages. 1992.

Vol. 377: A. Villar, Operator Theorems with Applications to Distributive Problems and Equilibrium Models. XVI, 160 pages. 1992.

Vol. 378: W. Krabs, J. Zowe (Eds.), Modern Methods of Optimization. Proceedings, 1990. VIII, 348 pages. 1992.

Vol. 379: K. Marti (Ed.), Stochastic Optimization. Proceedings, 1990. VII, 182 pages. 1992.

Vol. 380: J. Odelstad, Invariance and Structural Dependence. XII, 245 pages. 1992.

Vol. 381: C. Giannini, Topics in Structural VAR Econometrics. XI, 131 pages. 1992.

Vol. 382: W. Oettli, D. Pallaschke (Eds.), Advances in Optimization. Proceedings, 1991. X, 527 pages. 1992.

Vol. 383: J. Vartiainen, Capital Accumulation in a Corporatist Economy. VII, 177 pages. 1992.

Vol. 385: J. Gardeazabal, M. Regúlez, The Monetary Model of Exchange Rates and Cointegration. X, 194 pages. 1992.

GPSR Compliance

The European Union's (EU) General Product Safety Regulation (GPSR) is a set of rules that requires consumer products to be safe and our obligations to ensure this.

If you have any concerns about our products, you can contact us on ProductSafety@springernature.com

In case Publisher is established outside the EU, the EU authorized representative is:

Springer Nature Customer Service Center GmbH
Europaplatz 3
69115 Heidelberg, Germany

Batch number: 10844827

Printed by Printforce, the Netherlands